HOW TO CAPITALIZE ON YOUR PERSONAL STYLE

Avoid the 9 Myths

POWERFUL PUBLIC SPEAKING

Loren D. Crane, Ph.D.

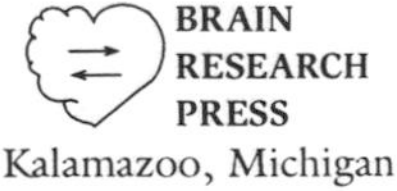

Kalamazoo, Michigan

Published by Brain Research Press
5175 Driftwood
Kalamazoo, MI 49009

Publisher's Cataloging-in-Publication Data
Crane, Loren D.
Powerful public speaking: how to capitalize on your personal style
/ Loren D. Crane. – Kalamazoo, Mich. :
Brain Research Press, 2000.

p. cm.

Includes bibliographical references and index.
ISBN: 0-9667330-0-2
1. Public speaking I. Title.
PN4121 .C73 2000 98-87547
808.5/1 – dc21 CIP

PROJECT COORDINATION BY JENKINS GROUP, INC.

03 02 01 00 * 5 4 3 2 1

Printed in the Unites States of America

POWERFUL PUBLIC SPEAKING

To my wife Marlene,
and our wonderful children:
Liann, Dan, Maren, and Kristin.

Foreword

Effective communication is the difference between the manager and the employee, the teacher and the student, the leader and the follower. You're in for a big treat. If you just opened this book you have made the most important step you can make to increase your value in the workplace and in your world.

What is so special about this book? Plenty! Unlike many books on speaking that simply quote great orators of the past and present, this book will make you into the great orator!

Loren D. Crane has taken every aspect of speaking and made it seem easy. Loren's approach has taken an intellectual look at standing in front of people and speaking. With this brilliant book we can evaluate the process of preparation, actually speaking and the eventual evaluation of what we have just done.

You will find endless value from Dr. Crane's life long experience as a leader among professional speakers. He has taken his life lessons and his work with thinking styles and combined them to give us a brilliant tool and a "must have" for any speaker's library. There is so much brilliance and wisdom in this book that it would be well for everyone – professional speaker, amateur speakers and others alike – to read every page.

When I have an important presentation I use this tool to raise the impact of my speech – the results speak for themselves! After reading this book I learned that if I could hire a tutor or coach to make me more effective it would have to be Dr. Loren D. Crane.

As a professional speaker, Loren has done it all, and he has given us a chronicle of success tactics. Even if you just need to give that "one speech," read this book, and get better at whatever you do –

as Loren lays out in this blueprint to success. You will be surprised by your results.

Thanks, Loren!

Michael Scott Karpovich
Certified Speaking Professional
Youngest president of the Professional Speakers Association of Michigan
Charter member of the Pennsylvania Speakers Association
Honorary lifetime member of the
New England Speakers Association
Second youngest Certified Speaking Professional in the world

Speeches can inspire, or they can corrupt. They can stir compassion, or they can inflame hatred. They can coerce allegiance through lies or they can authentically persuade through truth. Public speaking always involves ethical choices.

Fittingly, Loren D. Crane has made ethics an essential component of his "professional approach" to public speaking. Starting with the introduction of his model, Crane puts ethics front and center, unlike too many public speaking textbooks that relegate ethics to an afterthought in a chapter at the end.

Most significantly, Crane has emphasized ethics not only as a contributor to effectiveness, but as an inherent feature of the speaker-audience relationship. He demonstrates how important it is for the speaker to adopt a "servant-leader" attitude when delivering a speech – so that the audience's interests are primary, rather than the speaker's. This is an important insight, considering the extent to which the audience typically depends on the speaker's knowledge and good intentions.

By incorporating Crane's advice, you will be alerted to the ethical implications of each step of the speaking process: choosing subjects, organizing ideas, documenting evidence, adjusting to the audience and coping with nervousness. This book goes beyond what's customary and what works – it also pays attention to what makes you proud.

Sandra L. Borden
Center for the Study of Ethics in Society

True mastery of speaking skills is considered a necessary component to success in life. Written communication, while important, cannot begin to create the effect of the spoken word in emphasizing, persuading, or inciting someone to action. In today's competitive job market, the person with strong communication skills has a clear advantage over tongue-tied colleagues.

Some people have used the powers of speech to change the course of history. During World War II, Winston Churchill inspired his nation to stand up to the enemy and fight back. "These are not dark days; these are great days – the greatest days our country has ever lived," he thundered. These same words, spoken without power and passion or even arranged in a different order, would fall on deaf ears. While you may never be called upon to give a speech that would affect world history, you still may have the opportunity to give a speech that will influence others to take action or accept your ideas.

Giving a speech can be a nerve-racking – even frightening – experience, and writing one can be just as difficult. Most people do not know how to organize their thoughts and present them in a manner that will motivate or inspire the listener to act. Loren D. Crane's book, *Powerful Public Speaking: How to Capitalize on Your Personal Style*, clearly and concisely explains how to develop and present a speech. The book provides detailed, easy-to-follow instruction in speech preparation and delivery methods that anyone can use. Applying techniques from this book can erase fears commonly associated with public speaking and make you communicate your ideas easily and convincingly to any audience.

Ralph Waldo Emerson knew the value of competent public speaking. "Speech is power: speech is to persuade, to convert, to compel. It is to bring another out of his bad sense into your good sense." Use this book to learn how to develop and present powerful speeches that influence others to act.

Terrence J. McCann,
Executive Director
Toastmasters International

Contents

INTRODUCTION .... *xv*

PART I (Principles)

1 A PROFESSIONAL APPROACH 1
Myth of rhetoric
Social science
Personal effectiveness
Personal strengths
Personal ethics
Personal speech cycle decisions

2 LIVE SPEAKING SITUATIONS 5
Myth of attention factors
Attention
Perception
Language
Memory
Speech format

3 AUDIENCE DECISION MAKING 11
Myth of need-motivation
Decision making stages
Psychological continuum
Decision cycle stages

4 PREPARATION AND DELIVERY STYLES 15
Myth of preparation uniformity
Novice mistakes
Thinking styles
Personal strategies

PART II (Decisions)

5 GETTING SUBJECTS 19
Personal effectiveness decisions
Myth of demographic analysis
When asked to give a speech, what do I need to know?
How will I know when I have enough content?
Which of the four speech components should I select first?
What's most important in the speaker-audience relationship?

Whose interests come first in the relationship?
How do I determine audience interests?
How do I determine my interests?
How is the speech purpose related to content?
Which comes first, subject or purpose?
What's the best way to do research?

6 ORGANIZING PLANS 29
Personal effectiveness decisions
Myth of the logical outline
What's the purpose of organization?
How is content related to structure?
What are the different ways that ideas can relate to each other?
Why make an outline?
What's the idea-imagery outline?
What's the speech format?
What's the purpose of the introduction?
What's the purpose of the preview?
What's in the message of the speech?
How many ideas should be in a speech?
What's the purpose of the review?
What's the purpose of the conclusion?
What's a content plan?
What's a language plan?
What's a delivery plan?
What's an impromptu speech?

7 AIDING MEMORY 43
Personal effectiveness decisions
Myth of rote rehearsal
How do you combine idas with imagery in a context?
What's the best way to view a speech for purposes of memory?
What types of memory aid can I use?
Why should I use a language rehearsal?
What's the best way to rehearse language?
Why should I rehearse delivery?
What's the best way to rehearse delivery?

8 LOWERING STRESS 49
Personal effectiveness decisions
Myth of stage-fright
What can I expect?
What's the nature of stress?
How do I prepare mentally?
How do I prepare emotionally?
How do I prepare physically?
Why do I forget things when I stand up to speak?

9 SPEAKING 55
Personal effectiveness decisions
Myth of passive delivery

How can I reduce stress immediately prior to speaking?
Should I imagine the audience in an embarrasing situation?
Is there anything I can do during delivery to relieve stress?
How do I use delivery notes?
Does the speech purpose affect my delivery?
Do I really need to use gestures?
How do I improve my delivery?
I don't notice much audience feedback, why is that?
How can I learn to look at the audience?
How do I adapt to an audience?
What kind of adaptation can I make?
How do I evaluate myself after the speech?
What kind of speech assessment do I need from my audience?

PART III (Reference)

10 A PROFESSIONAL APPROACH 65
Myth of rhetoric
Social science
Personal effectiveness
Personal strengths
Personal ethics
Personal speech cycle decisions

11 LIVE SPEAKING SITUATIONS 71
Myth of attention factors
Attention
Perception
Language
Memory
Speech format

12 AUDIENCE DECISION MAKING 79
Myth of need-motivation
Decision making stages
Psychological continuum
Forms and functions

13 PREPARATION AND DELIVERY STYLES 91
Myth of preparation uniformity
Novice mistakes
Thinking styles
Personal effectiveness decisions

14 GETTING SUBJECTS 99
Personal effectiveness decisions
Myth of demographic analysis
Audience image
Four speech components
Speaker-audience relationship
Resource search

15 ORGANIZING PLANS 111
Personal effectiveness decisions
Myth of the logical outline
Content plan
Awareness speech
Information speech
Argument speech
Action speech
Speech purpose adaptation
Idea-imagery outline
Speech format plan
Language plan
Delivery plan
Impromptu speech

16 AIDING MEMORY 143
Personal effectiveness decisions
Myth of rote rehearsal
Delivery notes
Visual aid(s)
Mental pictures content rehearsal
Language rehearsal
Delivery rehearsal

17 LOWERING STRESS 153
Personal effectiveness decisions
Myth of stage-fright
Speech stress
Individual differences
Mental preparation
Emotional preparation
Physical preparation

18 SPEAKING 169
Personal effectiveness decisions
Myth of passive delivery
Coping
Audience adaptation
Requisite variety
Audience involvement
Speaking
Evaluating

ENDNOTES 183

DIRECTORY OF PROFESSIONAL SPEECH COACHES 193

TOASTMASTERS INTERNATIONAL 201

WORD INDEX 203

NAME INDEX 205

SPEECH PROGRESS CHART 207

Introduction

The truth is – most speeches are boring!

The first reason is that most speakers read their speeches. That's because they think they have to either memorize or read their speech, and for most people reading is easier. They feel memorization or reading is necessary to cope with a speaking situation which is fearful – stage fright, right?

Another reason speeches are boring is the organization – most are arranged in a deductive pattern because people think they must use a logical outline. That is also closely related to the belief that there is only one correct way to prepare a speech.

And still another reason is that their speech sounds like a written article. That's because they don't understand the difference between the written idiom and the speaking idiom.

Even more problems occur because speakers believe that the way to get a subject is to analyze the demographic features of the audience, and they believe that they can hold interest if they emphasize "factors of attention," plus they believe they can motivate people to action with a pattern of need-satisfaction.

Then, they practice by repeating their speech over and over and think they're ready to speak. And they also think they shouldn't move their hands or feet because it would be distracting.

The truth is – those beliefs are all myths!

The great enemy of the truth is often not the lie – deliberate, contrived, and dishonest, but the myth – persistent, persuasive, and unrealistic. – J. F. Kennedy

Some of those ideas come from rhetoric, some come from outdated theories of psychology, and others are the result of inexperience in speaking.

When circumstances change over time, but ideas don't you have a myth. A myth is a partial truth, which may work for some people, or in some situations – but for other people, and at other times, it doesn't work at all.

Eliminate nine major myths of public speaking to become a more professional speaker.

1) The myth of rhetoric
2) The myth of attention factors
3) The myth of need-motivation
4) The myth of preparation uniformity
5) The myth of demographic analysis
6) The myth of the logical outline
7) The myth of rote rehearsal
8) The myth of stage-fright
9) The myth of passive delivery

The most important truth about public speaking is – when a speaker capitalizes on personal strengths his or her speaking becomes authentic and effective.

Part one of this book is an outline of the major principles you need to understand before you begin preparing a speech. They are based on modern social science.

Part two consists of the decisions you make when preparing a speech. It reveals the strategies of people with different preparation and delivery styles.

Part three is a reference. It provides background for the principles and steps in speech preparation and delivery.

An individual could use this book as a text in a public speaking class or for personal study.

How I learned about the myths.

I received my B.A. in Speech from Brigham Young University and both my M.A. in Rhetoric and Ph.D. in Speech Education from the Ohio State University. My experience comes from over 30 years of teaching public speaking to university students, over a hundred paid presentations to large audiences, many more unpaid presentations, membership in the National Communication Association – the organization of academic professionals, and membership in the National Speakers Association – the organization of professional speakers.

Part I, Chapter 1

A Professional Approach

1

MYTH OF RHETORIC

This myth is that the principles taught by early rhetoricians are equally effective today. The alternative to this myth is modern social science. Social science includes knowledge of personal effectiveness, personal strengths, personal ethics, and personal speech cycle decisions.

SOCIAL SCIENCE

We have more knowledge about communication than ever before and it corrects many earlier concepts.

Comprehensive. Social science is the process of searching for greater correspondance between theory and practice which makes possible the effectiveness of more people in more situations.

Self-correcting. Social science does not rest on a static collection of knowledge, but is a process of continual discovery.

Three domains. The social science of public speaking is a search to understand the psychological realities of: a speaking situation, an audience, and a speaker.

Figure 1-1

PUBLIC SPEAKING REALITIES

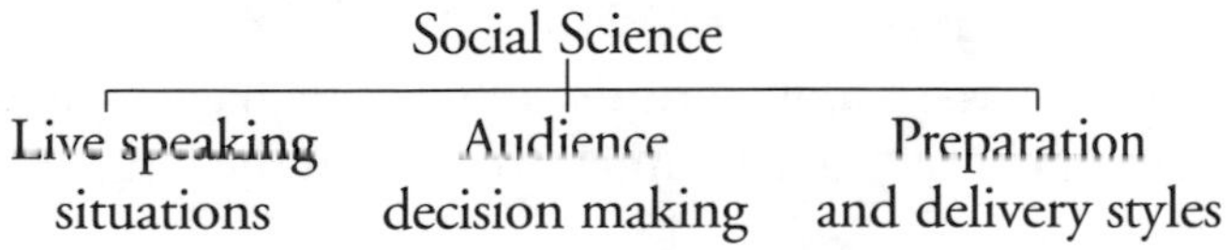

Social Science

Live speaking situations | Audience decision making | Preparation and delivery styles

Principle: A professional continually searches for the best information available about speaking situations, decision making, and preparation and delivery styles.

PERSONAL EFFECTIVENESS

A professional knows that typically, 80% of a person's effectiveness is the result of 20% of his or her actions. Thus, a professional focuses on the most important speaking tasks.

Figure 1-2
80-20 PRINCIPLE

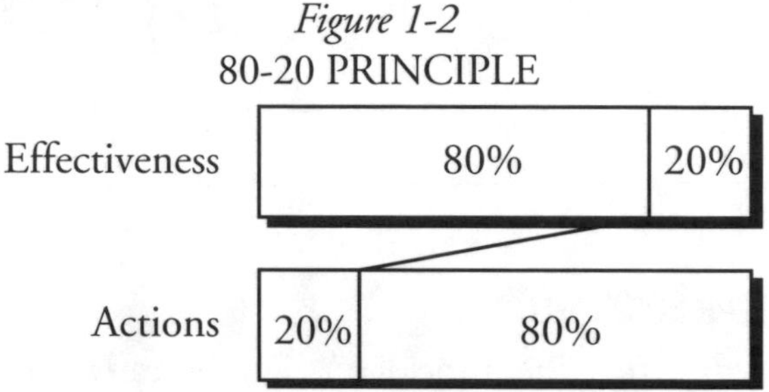

Principle: A professional identifies the most critical tasks and spends most of his or her time working on them.

PERSONAL STRENGTHS

A professional knows that different people have different talents, and speakers are most effective when they lead from their strengths.

Table 1-1
THINKING STYLES

Thinking	Feeling
Sensing	Intuition
Judgment	Perception
Auditory	Visual
etc.	etc.

Principle: A professional capitalizes on personal strengths.

PERSONAL ETHICS

The primary motivation of speakers should be to help people in an audience make better decisions. An ethical speaker will be perceived as having more integrity in delivery, have more self-confidence in delivery, and be more effective in the long term.

Table 1-2
ETHICAL MOTIVATION

Speaking integrity

Confident delivery

Long range effectiveness

Principle: *A professional is ethical, which increases personal effectiveness.*

PERSONAL SPEECH CYCLE DECISIONS

Public speaking consists of a complex system of skills.

Cycle. Public speaking is a reoccuring system of decision making.

Stages. A decision made at one stage affects all other stages.

Figure 1-3
THE SPEECH CYCLE

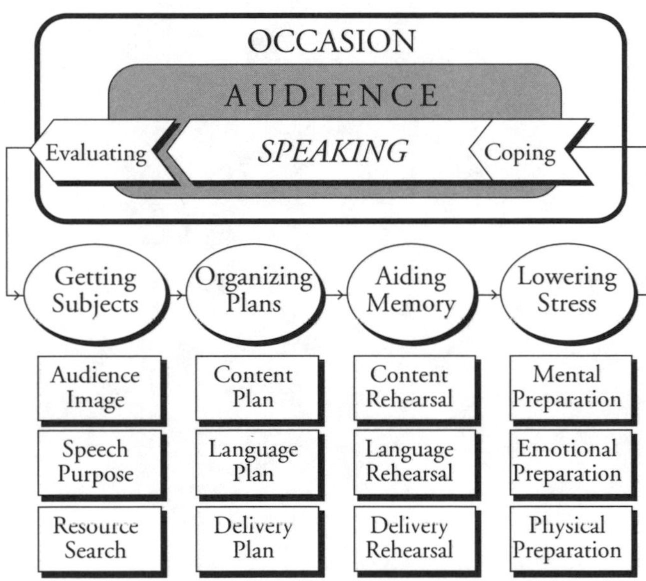

Principle: *A professional has a dynamic view of the complexity of public speaking.*

Part I, Chapter 2

Live Speaking Situations

MYTH OF ATTENTION FACTORS

This myth is that certain factors (activity, reality, proximity, familiarity, novelty, etc.) will hold the attention of an audience. The alternative to this myth is to be aware of the psychological constraints of listeners. These constraints are: attention, perception, language, and memory.

ATTENTION

Conversational limit. In our culture conversations between individuals average about four minutes, whether between a friend, stranger, or spouse. That comfort zone is an interactive situation, so listening to a speech even for four minutes is a greater stretch. You overcome this limit by the relevance of your message.

Figure 2-1
CONVERSATIONAL LIMIT

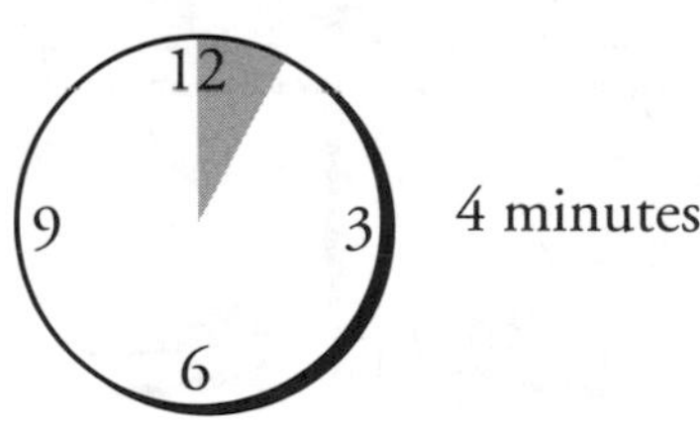

Sustained attention limit. A person's ability to sustain attention is approximately 40 seconds. You overcome this limit by the originality of your message.

Figure 2-2
SUSTAINED ATTENTION LIMIT

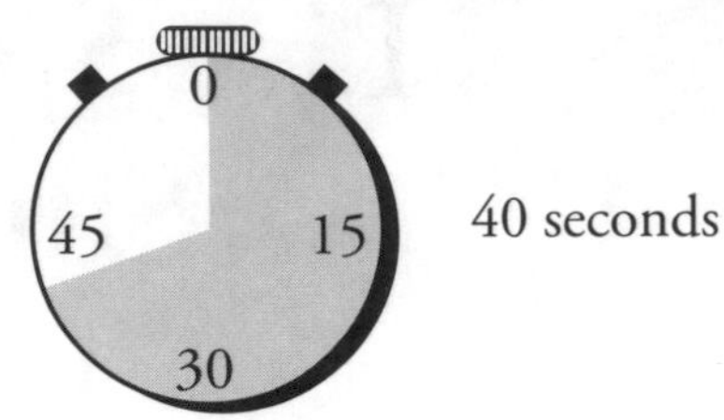

Change is primary. The nervous system is designed so that perception of change takes precedence over a constant stimulus.

Figure 2-3
CHANGE IS PRIMARY

***Principle:** A professional is relevant, original, and provides change to continually recapture attention of the audience.*

PERCEPTION

The perception of credibility is determined primarily by two variables, expertise and trust.

Figure 2-4
SPEAKER CREDIBILITY

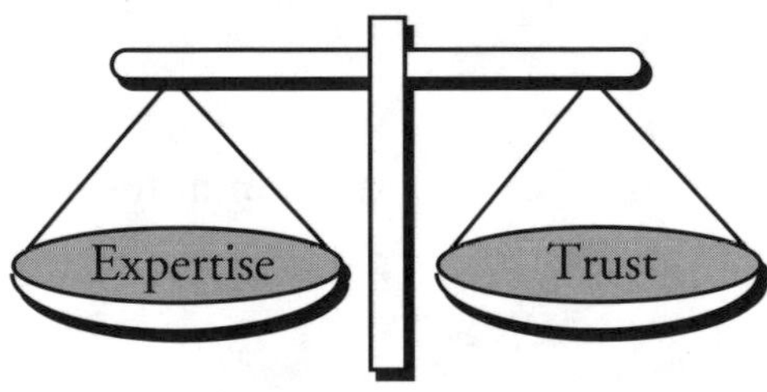

Expertise. Expertise means the speaker has relevant experience or has researched the subject. Speakers must cite their experience or cite their source of information.

Trust. Trust means listeners believe the speaker is honest. Speakers gain trust by self-disclosure and verbal-nonverbal consistency as shown in the perception pyramid.

Perception pyramid. Verbal-nonverbal consistency means that words, voice, and movement are integrated. The nonverbal cues must fit the words. If not, the nonverbal is believed and the speaker is judged a phoney. The more complex or controversial the message the more critical is the nonverbal.

Figure 2-5
PERCEPTION PYRAMID

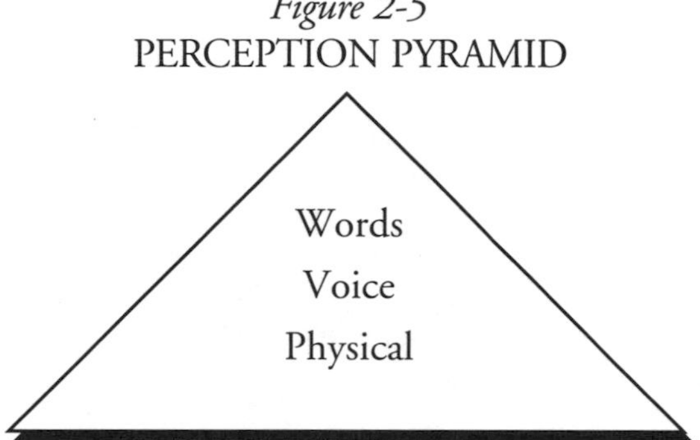

***Principle:** A professional establishes credibility by experience, sources, self-disclosure, and nonverbal consistency.*

LANGUAGE

The basic structure of verbal speech is significantly different from written language. The major features are: juxtaposition, redundancy, informality, and delivery.

Juxtaposition. Juxtaposition means that one idea is placed next to another idea in the simplest way possible.

Figure 2-6
JUXTAPOSITION

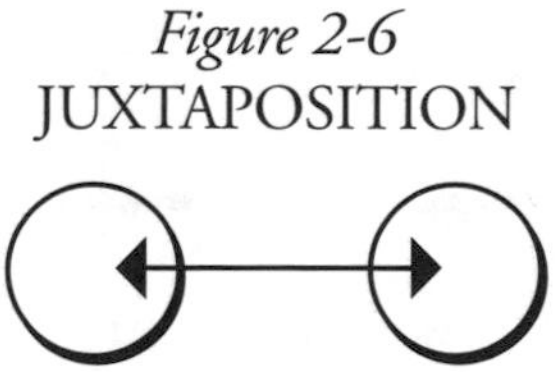

Redundancy. Redundancy means repetition. Important ideas need to be repeated several times.

Table 2-1
REDUNDANCY
Repetition
Repetition
Repetition

Informality. An immediate audience relationship is emphasized by personal language (personal pronouns).

Table 2-2
INFORMALITY
I YOU WE US

Delivery. Effective delivery (movement, gesture, and voice) must have variety.

Figure 2-7
DELIVERY

Principle: *A professional understands spoken English has simple structure, frequent repetition, personal language, and variety in delivery.*

MEMORY

On average, approximately 1/4 of your message will be remembered the next day. Since most of your speech will be forgotten, you must help the audience remember the most important parts of your message.

Figure 2-8
NEXT DAY MEMORY

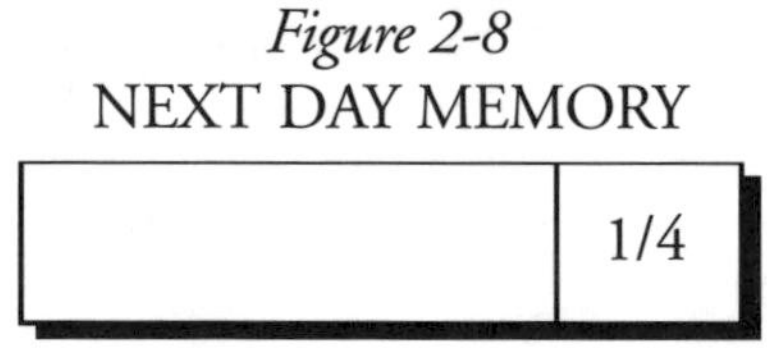

Number of points. The limits of short term memory are seven plus or minus two. On average, a person remembers about seven things at one time. Under poor conditions, the number drops to five and under good conditions it can be increased to nine.

Because of distractions in the speaking situation, a speech is near the low end of that formula.

Table 2-3
NUMBER OF POINTS MEMORY
7 ± 2

Position. Information at the end of a message is remembered best, nearly 100% (primacy effect). Next most important, is information at the beginning, about 70% recall (recency effect). The middle is remembered least, around 20%. But, anything which stands out as different will also be remembered (Von Restorff effect). Therefore, the key points of a message should stand out as different and also be repeated in the introduction and conclusion.

Figure 2-9
POSITION MEMORY

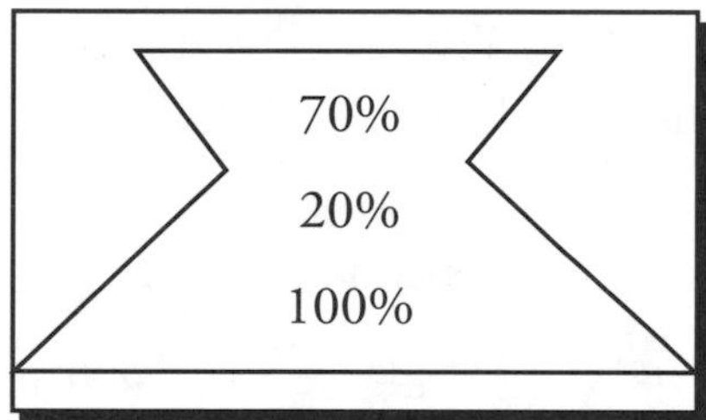

Abstract-concrete. Memory is facilitated by relating an idea to an image. Therefore, each main idea in a speech should be matched to some imagery.

Figure 2-10
ABSTRACT-CONCRETE MEMORY

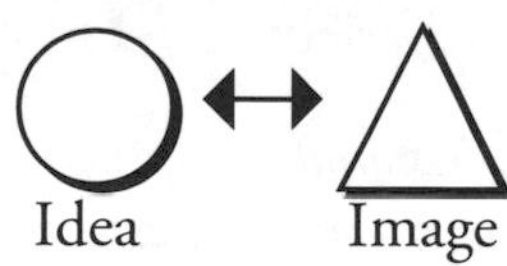

Emotion. Memory is facilitated by physiological arousal. Ideas or images associated with emotion will be remembered best. Therefore, emotive language and delivery emphasis are necessary.

Figure 2-11
EMOTION MEMORY

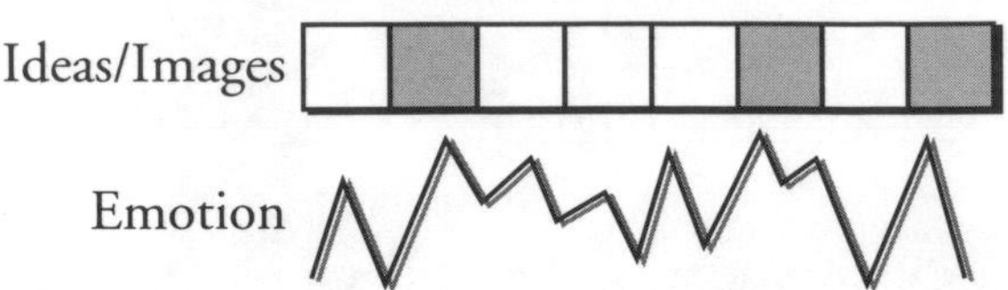

Principle: *A professional facillitates memory by design of the speech: few points, primacy, recency, difference, idea-imagery, emotive language, and delivery emphasis.*

SPEECH FORMAT

The foregoing psychological realities result in a pattern of speech organization designed to fit live speaking situations.

Table 2-4
SPEAKING REALITIES AND SPEECH FORMAT

Attention	Perception	Language	Memory	Format
Relevant				***Introduction***
		Repetition	Primacy	***Preview***
Original	Experience	Simple	Few points	***Message***
	Sources	Repetition	Idea-Imagery	
	Self-disclosure	Personal	Difference	
			Emotive lang.	
		Repetition	Recency	***Review***
Relevant				***Conclusion***
Changes	Nonverbal	Variety	Emphasis	***Delivery***

Principle: *A professional understands why a speech has a simple structure.*

Part I, Chapter 3

Audience Decision Making

MYTH OF NEED-MOTIVATION

This myth is that satisfying people's needs will motivate them to take the action you recommend. The alternative is focusing on decision making stages.

DECISION MAKING STAGES

Models of effective communication rest on the premise of how people think and a model of decision making is the most relevant model for public speaking. Such a model can be generalized from current research.

Figure 3-1
DECISION MAKING

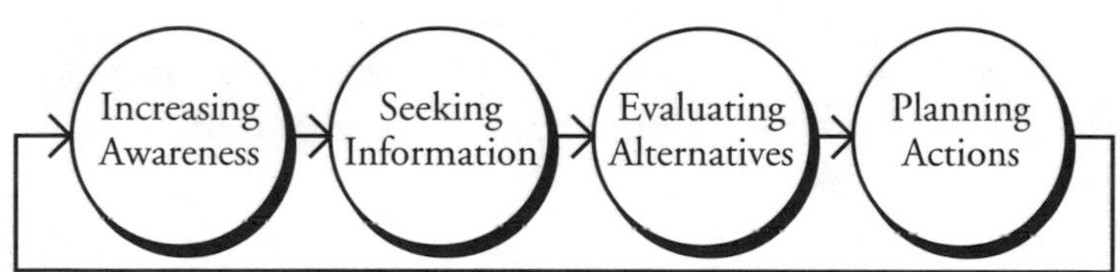

Purpose model. The decision making stages can be generalized to an audience. Thus, each stage can be a model for a speech purpose: awareness, information, argument, action.

Figure 3-2
SPEECH PURPOSES

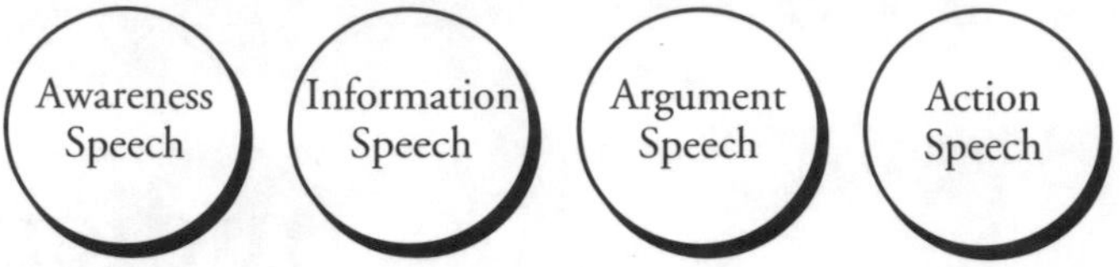

Awareness Speech — Information Speech — Argument Speech — Action Speech

***Principle:** A professional matches decision making stages to speech purposes.*

PSYCHOLOGICAL CONTINUUM

There is a natural relationship between stages of decision making and psychological concepts.

Awareness. The purpose is to change priorities.
Information. The purpose is to change beliefs.
Argument. The purpose is to change attitudes.
Action. The purpose is to change behaviors.

Table 3-1
SPEECH CONTINUUM

Speech	Focus
Awareness	Priorities
Information	Beliefs
Argument	Attitudes
Action	Behaviors

Psychological concepts also progressively build on each other.

Priority. A ranking of importance.

Belief. A ranking of importance plus what is true or not true.

Attitude. A ranking of importance plus what is true or not true plus for or against.

Behavior. A ranking of importance plus what is true or not true plus for or against plus acting or not taking action.

Table 3-2

PSYCHOLOGICAL CONTINUUM

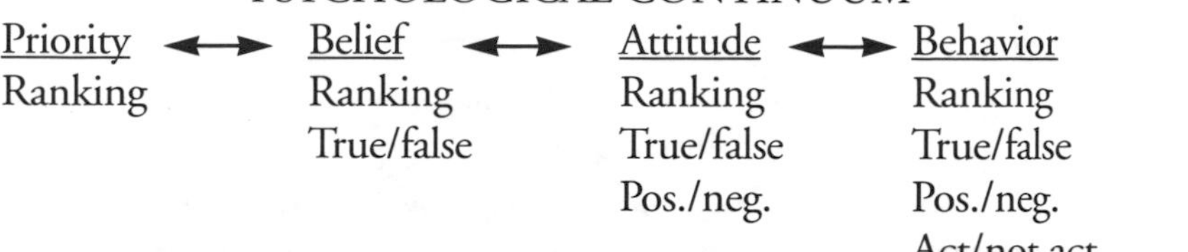

Priority ⟷	Belief ⟷	Attitude ⟷	Behavior
Ranking	Ranking	Ranking	Ranking
	True/false	True/false	True/false
		Pos./neg.	Pos./neg.
			Act/not act

***Principle:** A professional uses speech purposes to determine speech structure and content.*

The assumption is that most of the audience would benefit if a certain question were answered.

Awareness. The question is, "What is important?"

Information. The question is, "What is it?"

Argument: The question is, "What is best?"

Action: The question is, "What should I do?"

Table 3-3

SPEECH PURPOSE DESIGN

Speech	Question
Awareness	What is important?
Information	What is it?
Argument	What is best?
Action	What should I do?

DECISION CYCLE STAGES

Listening consists of a complex system of skills.

Cycle. Listening is a reoccuring system of decision making.

Stages. A decision made at one stage affects all other stages.

Figure 3-3
THE DECISION CYCLE

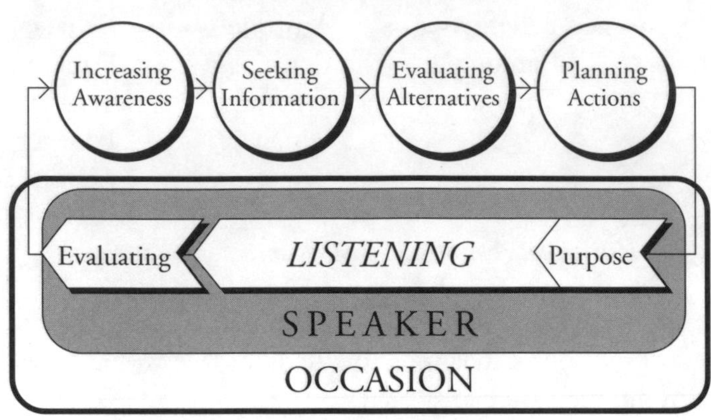

Principle: *A professional has a dynamic view of the complexity of decision making.*

Part I, Chapter 4

Preparation and Delivery Styles

MYTH OF PREPARATION UNIFORMITY

This myth is that there is one best way for all speakers to prepare speeches. The alternative is that speakers have different thinking styles.

NOVICE MISTAKES

One reason for poor speaking is because of inexperience. Common mistakes are:

Searching too long for a super subject,
Relying on a great article,
Copying ideas, organization, and language verbatim.

This leads to problems later, because it makes it more difficult for a speaker to:

Remember the speech,
Have effective delivery,
Adapt to the audience.

Principle: *A professional understands how to create an authentic speech and develop an authentic relationship with an audience.*

THINKING STYLES

Another reason for poor speaking is that a speaker has not identified his or her personal thinking strengths.

Two hemispheres. Thinking is primarily a function of the two cerebral hemispheres of the brain. One hemisphere function is serial processing of information, the other hemisphere function is parallel processing.

Thinking Bias. Individual differences form a normal curve. Some individuals have a strong bias toward one brain function compared to the other. Some people have only a moderate bias, and for others, the two styles of thinking are about equally easy to use.

Figure 4-1
THINKING BIAS

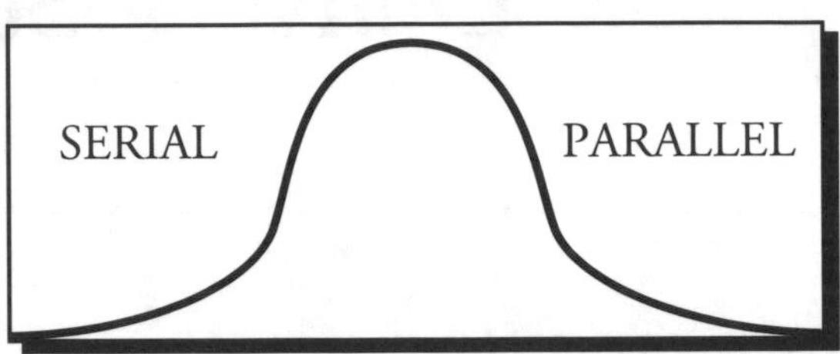

Opposite patterns. A bias toward one style of thinking means that some tasks will be difficult for you and other tasks will be easy. You need to discover for each speaking task whether you have a bias or whether you can use either opposite style.

Table 4-1
OPPOSITE PATTERNS

Serial	Parallel
Sequencing	Correlating
Deductive	Inductive
Systematic	Intuitive
Monopath	Polypath
etc.	etc.

Principle: *A professional speaker knows his or her personal thinking style in each stage of speech preparation and delivery.*

PERSONAL STRATEGIES

Many beginning speakers who have difficulty with some speech preparation and delivery tasks conclude that they can't be effective speakers. They don't know that speakers can approach speaking tasks in different ways.

Opposite styles. To make it easier to identify your personal speaking strategies, this book contrasts opposite styles. Experiment to find where you are on the continuum between the two extremes. For one task, you may be at one extreme. For another task, you may be at the opposite end. For still another task, you may be in the middle. And for yet another task, you may be able to do it either of the two opposite ways.

Research. A survey of university public speaking students revealed important differences in preparation and delivery which are related directly to brain hemisphere thinking styles.

Table 4-2
PERSONAL STRATEGIES

Speech Cycle	Strategies
Getting Subjects	Reasoning vs Imagination
Organizing Plans	Logical vs Interesting
Aiding Memory	Words vs Pictures
Lowering Stress	Freeze vs Fidget
Speaking	Low energy vs High energy

***Principle:** Identify your personal strengths and capitalize on them.*

18

Part II, Chapter 5

Getting Subjects

Personal effectiveness decisions

- When getting a subject, I use my reasoning more than my imagination. (47%)
- When getting a subject, I use my imagination more than my reasoning. (36%)
- Equal. (17%)

- I tend to begin with a general subject and then think of specific ideas, examples, etc. (36%)
- I tend to begin with an idea or example and then define the subject. (23%)
- I sometimes do it deductively, sometimes inductively. (41%)

- To understand an audience I analyze age, sex, religion, politics, etc. (15%)
- To understand an audience I imagine their thoughts, feelings, problems, etc. (36%)
- I believe the audience will be interested in a subject which interests me. (49%)

- I find it difficult to think of a speech subject. (41%)
- I think of many subjects, and have trouble choosing. (37%)
- Other. (22%)

- It's easier to choose a subject first before choosing a purpose. (56%)

- It's easier to choose a purpose first before choosing a subject. (44%)

- It takes me longer to choose a subject, than to organize it. (55%)
- It takes me longer to organize a subject, than to choose it. (37%)
- Equal. (8%)

Myth of demographic analysis

This myth is that knowing audience demographics – sex, age, socioeconomic level, etc. – will help you choose a subject. The alternative is the speaker-audience relationship.

When asked to give a speech, what do I need to know?

Start with the memory of your last speech. Take a moment to remember what aspects went well and what aspects you would like to improve.

First, gather all the information you can about the audience, the occasion, and the location.

Why did they ask you?
Who are the people in the audience?
How many will be in the audience?
What is the nature of the occasion?
What expectations will the audience have?
How much time will you have? How strict are the time limits?
Are microphones available, overhead projectors, etc?
Will someone introduce you, if so, who?
etc.

Second, create an image in your mind of the people, occasion, and location of the speech.

Third, getting a subject consists of completing four tasks – there are four speech components.

How will I know when I have enough content?

The four components of a speech are: ideas, imagery, speech nucleus, and speech subject label.

Ideas are abstract statements about thoughts and feelings.

Figure 5-1
IDEAS

Imagery is a concrete statement: fact, example, quote, story, etc.

Figure 5-2
IMAGERY

The *speech nucleus* is the most important thought in the speech around which all other ideas and imagery are organized. Any idea or imagery that doesn't directly relate to your speech nucleus should be discarded. It is sometimes called the thesis.

Figure 5-3
SPEECH NUCLEUS

A *speech subject label* sets the limits on how broad your subject is, given the amount of time you have. Any idea or imagery that doesn't fall within your subject label boundary should be discarded.

Figure 5-4
SPEECH SUBJECT LABEL

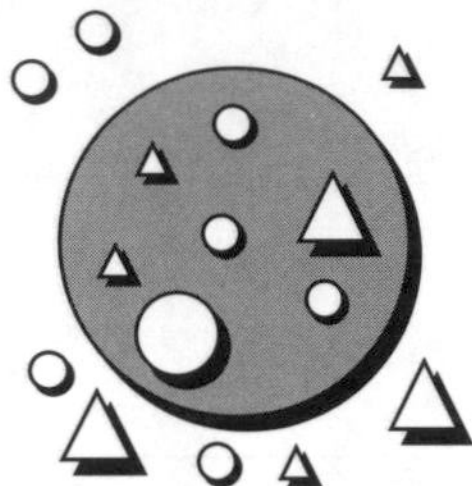

When you've gathered two kinds of information (ideas and imagery) and made two decisions (nucleus and label) you have all the components for your speech.

Which of the four speech components should I select first?

It doesn't matter, the four tasks can be completed in any order, but each one impacts the others.

Deductive approach. Start with a possible subject, then divide the subject up into what you know about it (ideas, imagery), and finally select what to put in your speech.

Figure 5-5
DEDUCTIVE APPROACH
General subject > divide into parts > decide what to use

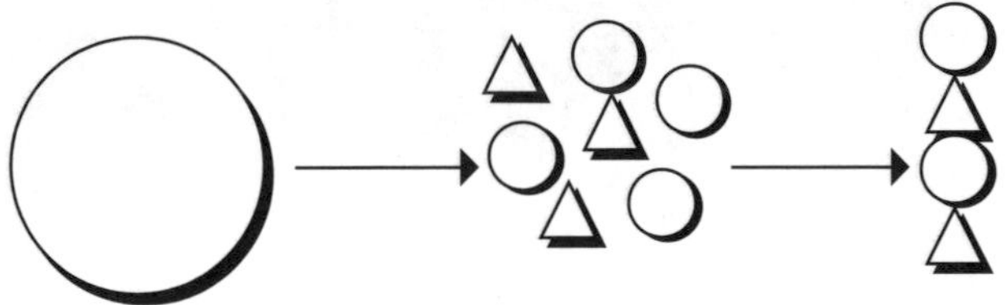

Inductive approach. Begin with a single idea, or imagery, add other related ideas and imagery, and finally select what to put into your speech.

Figure 5-6
INDUCTIVE APPROACH
One idea/image> add others > decide what to use

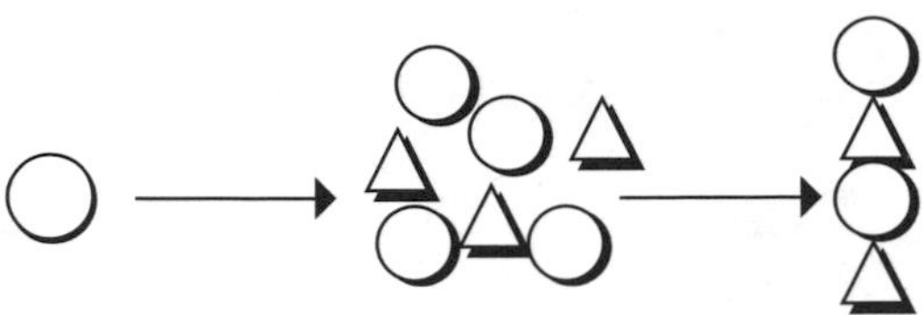

What's most important in the speaker-audience relationship?

Most important is whether or not you have spoken to them before. That makes a difference in how you prepare.

Table 5-1
TWO AUDIENCE TYPES

New audience Same speech	Same audience New speech
Improve organization/language	Choose all subjects at one time
Develop speaking skills	Develop a theme or more depth
Have increased confidence	Get to know audience better

Whose interests come first in the relationship?

Either one, but more importantly, your work goes back and forth continually. When you think of something to say, compare it to what you think the audience would like to hear. When you think of something you believe the audience would like to hear, com pare it to what you would like to say. Your content must satisfy both requirements.

Figure 5-7
SPEAKER-AUDIENCE RELATIONSHIP

Speaker-Image ↔ Audience-Image
↓
Ideas
Subjects
Imagery
Nucleus

How do I determine audience interests?

Demographic. Analyze characteristics of the audience like: sex, age, religion, politics, socio-economic level, etc. That's helpful information, but those judgments are stereotypes. They have value in a negative way – warning you what not to say that might offend someone.

Empathy. This has value in a positive way – it suggests subjects. Imagine one of the individuals in the audience. What would he or she be thinking and feeling? What would be his or her problems? How could you help that person? A listener probably has to make many of the same decisions that you have made. Imagine their interests in relationship to your interests.

How do I determine my interests?

Begin with a self inventory.

Table 5-2
SELF INVENTORY

Your speeches	Your work	Classes taken
Books read	Papers written	Skills
Travels	Goals	Curiosities
Decisions	Influences	Problems

Continue by using word probes to suggest possibilities. Here are some examples, but you can create your own probes.

Table 5-3
WORD PROBES

Occupation	Politics	Education	Business
	Religion	Farming	Sports
	Science	Medicine	Law
	Industry	Technology	Sales
People	Babies	Children	Youth
	Adults	Aged	Handicapped
	Genius	Dating	Genetics
	Birth	Marriage	Death

Media	TV	Newspapers	Radio
	Plays	Magazines	Books
	Movies	Arts	Music
	Dance	Computers	
Feeling	Hope	Love	Fear
	Hate	Happy	Disgust
	Boredom	Admire	Thrill
Social	City	Nation	Fashion
	Family	Leaders	Crime
	Money	Wars	Drugs
	History	Entertainment	Pollution
	Energy	Drinking	Tobacco
	U.N.	Minorities	Diseases
	Trade	Space	Guns
	Gambling	Culture	Transportation
Geographic	Asia	Africa	Europe
	So. America	No. America	Australia
	Islands	Middle east	Antartica
Question	Who	What	Why
	When	Where	How
Polarity	Wealth-Poverty	Success-Failure	Good-Bad
	Wise-Foolish	Empathy-Ridicule	New-Old
	Conserve-Waste	Part-Whole	Innocence-Guilt
	Theory-Practice	Humble-Proud	Conform-Rebel
	Similar-Different	Known-Unknown	Simple-Complex
	Cooperate-Compete	Increase-Decrease	Strong Weak

Take one set of probes and match it up with another set. Ask yourself if there is a possible speech subject, or idea, or imagery, or speech nucleus suggested by each match-up.

Figure 5-8
PROBE MATRIX EXAMPLE

	Known-Unknown	Free-Control	Anger-Apathy	Cause-Effect	Think-Feel	Positive-Negative
Religion						
Education						
Sports						
Science						
Business						
Politics						
Medicine						
Law						

How is the speech purpose related to content?

To change priorities you emphasize values.
To change beliefs you emphasize concepts.
To change attitudes you emphasize evidence.
To change behaviors you emphasize illustrations.

Table 5-4
SPEECH PURPOSES AND CONTENT

Speech	Focus	Content
Awareness	Priorities	Values
Information	Beliefs	Concepts
Argument	Attitudes	Evidence
Action	Behaviors	Illustrations

Which comes first, subject or purpose?

Either one. It doesn't matter.

Subject first. Pair a possible subject with different purposes.

Table 5-5
SUBJECT FIRST EXAMPLE

Subject ⟶	Purpose
Unions	Awareness
	Information
	Argument
	Action

Purpose first. Pair a possible speech purpose to different word probes.

Table 5-6
PURPOSE FIRST EXAMPLE

Purpose ⟶	Subject
Information	Psychology
	Government
	World
	Consumers

What's the best way to do research?

The two most important criteria are accuracy and recency. They apply to a library-type search, an internet-type search, or interviews.

A *library* is basically a collection of reference works (encyclopedias, etc.), a collection of books (fiction and non-fiction), and a collection of periodicals (magazines, journals).

Reference works are very accurate, but some don't have the most recent information.

Books are usually accurate, but may not have the most recent information.

Popular periodicals have recent information, but may not be very accurate.

Professional periodicals are the most recent and the most accurate-this is your best source of print information.

Figure 5-9
PRINT RESOURCE EXAMPLES

READERS	Periodicals	Books	Reference
Limited Professional	Conference proceedings	Technical manual	Government census
General Professional	*Bulletin of Atomic Sci.*	Text books	*Education Index*
Limited Popular	*Psychology Today*	Hobbies	*Encyclopedia Britannica*
General Popular	*Reader's Digest*	Self-Improvement	*World Almanac*

Internet information is up-to-the-minute, but a lot of it may not be accurate. Unless you know the validity of the source, don't believe the information. Verify information from the internet with a second source.

Interviews are an excellent source of information. A comprehensive approach would be a well-structured survey of several people. A more targeted approach would be a single conversation with an expert.

When you have collected some ideas, collected some imagery, selected a general subject label, and selected a specific speech nucleus, you are ready to move on to organizing your speech.

Part II, Chapter 6

Organizing Plans

Personal effectiveness decisions

- I arrange the points in my speech in the most "logical" way. (42%)
- I arrange the points in my speech in the most "interesting" way. (39%)
- Equal. (19%)

- I plan and rearrange my points primarily on paper. (51%)
- I plan and rearrange my points primarily in my head. (43%)
- Equal. (6%)

- A logical outline helps me organize a speech. (37%)
- An idea-imagery outline helps me organize my speech. (30%)
- I don't use an outline to organize my speech. (33%)

- I examine my language and try to improve it for a speech. (37%)
- I use my natural expression. (63%)

- I plan how I'm going to deliver a speech. (58%)
- I don't plan my delivery. (42%)

Myth of the logical outline.

This is the belief that the logical outline is the best way to organize a speech. The alternative is the idea-imagery outline.

What's the purpose of organization?

Organization creates meaning. When relationships between ideas are clear, they are easy to understand and that makes them easy to remember, both for you, and for the audience.

How is content related to structure?

Awareness. The content is values, the structure is comparing.
Information. The content is concepts, the structure is clarifying.
Argument. The content is evidence, the structure is reasoning.
Action. The content is illustrations, the structure is motivating.

Table 6-1
CONTENT AND STRUCTURE OF SPEECHES

Speech	Content	Structure
Awareness	Values	Comparing
Information	Concepts	Clarifying
Argument	Evidence	Reasoning
Action	Illustrations	Motivating

Figure 6-1
PURPOSE AND ORGANIZATION

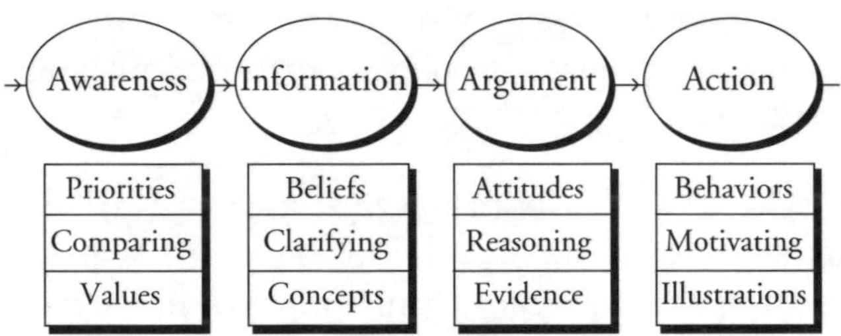

See a more detailed explanation in chapter 15.

What are the different ways that ideas can relate to each other?

There are only two patterns of relationship, but there is also a non-pattern.

Sequence. Some ideas follow each other in a natural sequence. It's easiesr to understand one idea if another idea comes first.

Figure 6-1
SEQUENCE PATTERN

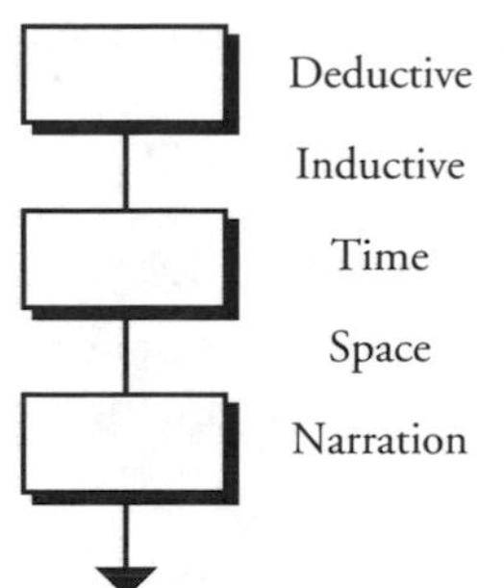

Deductive. A major point is listed first, and then the appropriate subparts, or implications come afterward.

Inductive. Many specifics are listed and then the appropriate conclusion, or synthesis is given.

Time. The natural chronological order of events or processes.

Space. Description of objects or places that follows a specific order – left to right, top to bottom, outside to inside, etc.

Narration. The telling of a story.

Correlation. Some ideas naturally go together. They are best understood in relationship to each other. Sometimes the two ideas contrast, other times they are similar. Sometimes one is a response to the other.

Figure 6-2
CORRELATION PATTERN

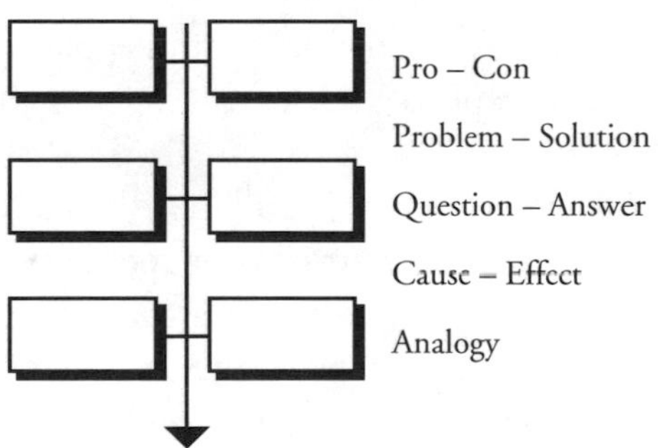

Pro-Con. Arguments in favor are contrasted with arguments against.

Problem-Solution. Each aspect of a problem is matched with a proposed solution.

Question-Answer. Each question is followed by an appropriate answer.

Cause-Effect. The relationship between a cause and its effect is explained, or an effect is traced back to its cause.

Analogy. Similarities and/or differences are compared.

Selection. Sometimes ideas relate to each other without sequence or correlation. That means you could remove one idea without changing the relationships between the others, or add a new idea without affecting the relationships between the others. Changing the order of the ideas would still not make a difference. Therefore, you may arbitrarily select which ideas you want and also select the order you want.

Figure 6-3
SELECTION PATTERN

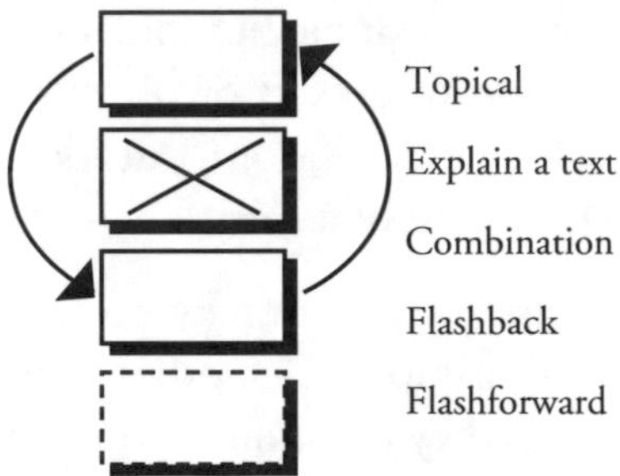

Topical. All the ideas relate to the same subject, but the ideas are simply a list. A description of something without any particular order.

Explain a text. State a definition and explain each word. Select a quotation and explain each part. Create a theme and explain related ideas, etc.

Combination. Sometimes you'll need to combine two or more patterns. Maybe the first part of your speech consists of ideas in a sequence, then you have some ideas that are naturally matched. Or, perhaps you start with two paired ideas and then you have a simple list of ideas, then you have two ideas that go together, etc.

Flashback. Suppose you are aware that necessary background material or preliminary information at the beginning of your speech is boring. You could start somewhere in the middle at an interesting point and then later go back to fill in the necessary material before continuing.

Table 6-2
FLASHBACK

Natural order	Revised order
Past history (weak)	Present problem
Present problem	Past history
Future solutions	Future solutions

Flashforward. The flashforward technique allows you to substitute more interesting material at the end of the speech. For example, in a speech about technology you could begin with the present applications of knowledge and then jump to future technological possibilities before explaining current knowledge which would make possible the future you predict.

Table 6-3
FLASHFORWARD

Natural order	Revised order
Present technology	Present technology
Present knowledge	Future technology
Future technology (weak)	Present knowledge

Why make an outline?

An outline helps you decide: 1) the order of ideas, 2) the matching of ideas to imagery, and 3) whether the idea or the imgery should come first. You could use a traditional outline which emphasizes logical order or you could use an idea-imagery outline which is more flexible.

The logical preparation outline can be used for any speech. It has a deductive structure.

Table 6-4
LOGICAL PREPARATION OUTLINE

I. First main point
  A. Subdivision of main point
  B. Subdivision of main point
    1. Further division
    2. Further division
II. Second main point
etc.

Coordination and subordination are the two principles which govern the creation of the logical outline.

Coordination

a) The subject is divided into ideas which are of equal generality.
b) Only one principle of division or classification may be used.
c) The divisions must exhaust the subject with nothing left over.
d) All ideas at the same level of generality are given the same type of symbol.

Subordination

a) Each idea may be subdivided into more specific ideas.
b) Each division must result in at least two more specific ideas.
c) Supporting material may be grouped under an idea.
d) The symbols change in the following order: Roman numerals, capital letters, Arabic numerals, lower case letters, Arabic numerals with a parenthesis, lower case letters with a parenthesis. Most outlines don't go beyond five divisions.

As an example, note the following which is the first part of a speech entitled, "Organizational Communication: State of the Art."[1] Complete sentences are used in this example.

Table 6-5

EXAMPLE OF A LOGICAL PREPARATION OUTLINE

I. The age of "future shock" is upon us.
   A. We are all subjected to instant travel, instant change and instant communication.
      1. Today we can send a man to the moon in less time than it takes for a paracel post package to travel from Boston to San Franscisco.
      2. Within five minutes we can talk on the telephone to almost any part of the world.
      3. Satellite networks enable us to be eyewitness observers at the funeral of a world leader, the landing of a spaceship on the moon, or even a full-scale war – without ever leaving our living rooms.

   B. Despite many space age communication victorys, however, we still witness the moral decay of our government and political institutions, the disintegration of our families, and the bankruptcy of our businesses.

1. It appears that advances in technological communication are not positively related to successful interpersonal communication.
2. In fact, the relationship between the two may be inverse.

C. In 1956 William Whyte labeled most of us organization men because of the large amount of time we spend within organizations.

1. In 1973, Harry Levinson claimed that this is still true, that 90% of those who work do so in organizations.

etc.

What's the idea-imagery outline?

The idea-imagery preparation outline can be used for any speech.

Table 6-6

IDEA-IMAGERY PREPARATION OUTLINE

Ideas	Imagery
Abstract statements	Concrete statements

The principles which govern the creation of the idea-imagery outline are:

a) Write out introduction word-for-word.
b) Draw a dotted line to separate the introduction from the rest of the speech.
c) Divide the paper with a vertical line down the middle.
d) Write idea statements on the left side of the center line and imagery statements on the right side.
e) The statements may appear consecutively in any order. Put each one on a separate line so the order is obvious.
f) Draw another dotted line before the conclusion.
g) Write out the conclusion word-for-word.

Here is the same speech on organizational communication in the idea-imagery structure.

Table 6-7
EXAMPLE OF AN IDEA-IMAGERY PREPARATION OUTLINE

The age of "future shock" is upon us.

We are all subjected to instant travel, instant change and instant communication.

....

Today we can send a man to the moon in less time than it takes for a paracel post package to travel from Boston to San Franscisco.

Within five minutes we can talk on the telephone to almost any part of the world.

Satellite networks enable us to be eyewitness observers at the funeral of a world leader, the landing of a spaceship on the moon, or even a full-scale war – without ever leaving our living rooms.

Despite many space age communication victorys, however, we still witness the moral decay of our government and political institutions, the disintegration of our families, and the bankruptcy of our businesses.

It appears that advances in technological communication are not positively related to successful interpersonal communication.

In fact, the relationship between the two may be inverse.

In 1956 William Whyte labeled most of us organization men because of the large amount of time we spend within organizations.

In 1973, Harry Levinson claimed that this is still true, that 90% of those who work do so in organizations.

etc.

Obviously, this outline could consist of just phrases or words instead of complete sentences.

Use the organizational aid with which you are most comfortable.

What's the speech format?

The speech format is: introduction, preview, message, review, conclusion.

Table 6-8
SPEECH FORMAT
Introduction (Why)
Preview (What)
Message (Ideas & Imagery)
Review (What)
Conclusion (Why)

What's the purpose of the introduction?

It answers the listener's question, "Why should I listen to this speech?" You create interest.

Table 6-9
INTRODUCTION EXAMPLES

A claim	A question
A joke	A warning
A plea	A description
A story	An hypothesis
An example	A fact
A quotation	A statistic
A definition	A compliment
etc.	

What's the purpose of the preview?

It answers the listener's question, "What is the speech going to be about?" You explain what your main points are or what your purpose is.

Table 6-10
PREVIEW EXAMPLES
My main points are....
My purpose is....
My text is....

What's in the message of the speech?

Ideas and imagery. Ideas are abstract statements about what you think and how you feel. Imagery is divided into evidence and illustrations. Evidence consists of facts, statistics, and expert testimony. Illustrations are examples, stories, and quotations.

How many ideas should be in a speech?

Five or fewer if you explain each of them in detail. You can cover more if the discussion of each is brief.

What's the purpose of the review?

It's a reminder of "what" the speech was about. It's a repetition of the preview, you summarize your main points or purpose.

What's the purpose of the conclusion?

It tells the audience "why" they should remember your speech. It may refer back to your introduction. You focus again on the importance of your message.

What's a content plan?

The overall organization is dictated first by speech purpose. Then comes idea patterns. That is followed by outlining. And finally the speech format is created.

Table 6-11

ORGANIZATION SUMMARY

Purpose >>	Idea patterns >>	Outline >>	Format
(Decision making research)	(Information processing research)	(Thinking style research)	(Situation constraints research)
Awareness	Sequence	Order	Introduction
Information	Correlation	Matching	Preview
Argument	Selection	Lead	Message
Action			Review
			Conclusion

What's a language plan?

A language plan is the decisions you make about your choice of words. Below are some of the more important ones.

Pronunciation. If you have any doubts about how a word is pronounced check with someone or look it up.

Grammar. Ask someone to listen for grammatical errors in your speech.

Explanation. The logical, scientific, exact usage of language may be necessary for your speech or some part of it.

Description. The poetic, colorful, suggestive, vivid usage of language may be necessary for your speech or some part of it.

Slang. Slang often needs to be defined, some in the audience may not understand.

Definition. Technical terms of course need to be defined.

Humor. An asset if it relates directly to your subject.

Figures of speech. They are created by comparison and repetition. Freely use metaphorical techinques. Freely use parallel structure.

Oratory. Find the language to express what others are feeling, but can't put into words.

What's a delivery plan?

A delivery plan matches vocal and physical emphasis to your ideas and imagery.

Decreasing interest. The natural pattern is for audience interest to decrease.

Figure 6-4
EXAMPLE OF AUDIENCE INTEREST

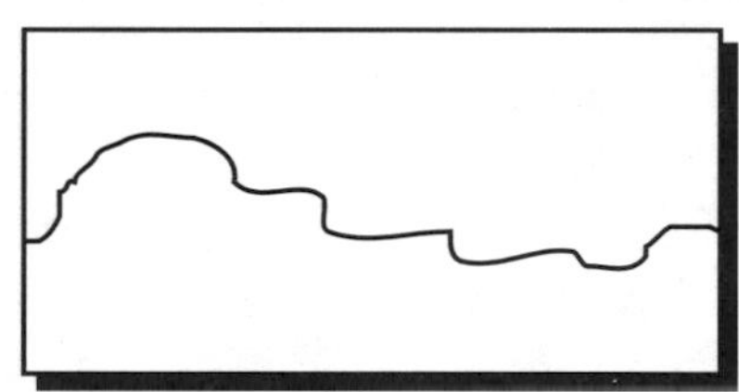

Planned Emphasis. Decide before speaking, which ideas or imagery should be emphasized. One example would be to emphasize the introduction and conclusion more than the points in the body.

Figure 6-5
EXAMPLE OF PLANNED EMPHASIS

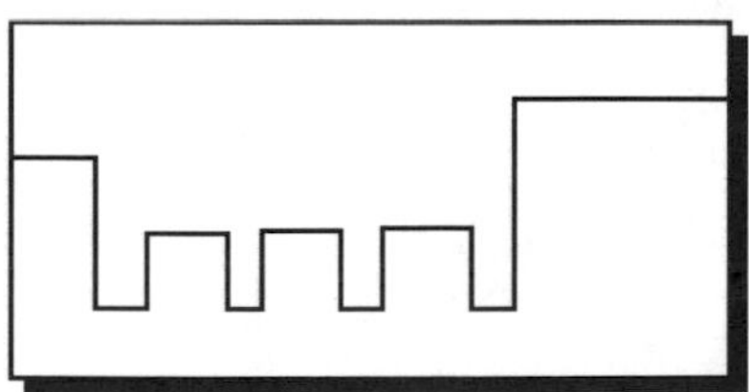

Another example would progressively build emphasis throughout the speech.

Figure 6-6
EXAMPLE OF PLANNED EMPHASIS

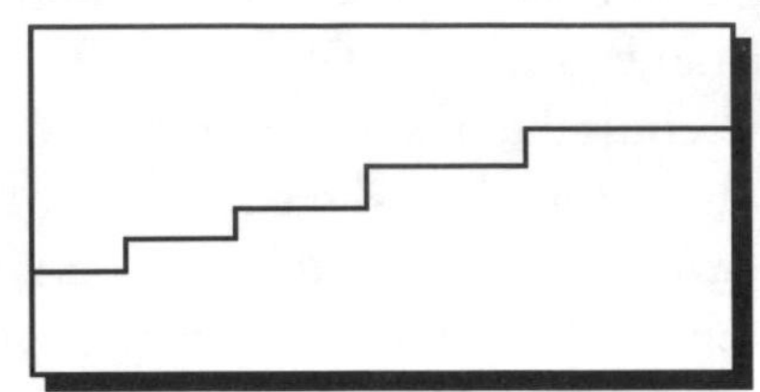

Be sure to emphasize your speech nucleus.

Planned Alternatives. Also decide where you could change, or cut, or add material, if it became necessary.

Table 6-12
PLANNED ALTERNATIVES EXAMPLE

Format	Decision
Introduction	Could change
Preview	Don't change
1st point	Don't change
2nd point	Could lengthen
3rd point	Could shorten
Review	Could shorten
Conclusion	Don't change

What's an impromptu speech?

Impromptu speaking is a simplified version of all speaking. Impromptu is the name of a speech that is given when you have only a minute or two to prepare and you only speak for a minute or two. It should consist of one clearly presented idea.

Structure first. Create or find a pattern that works for you and then plug information into that framework. For example, take the pattern: "On the topic... I think... Because... Thank you."

Then you fill in the blanks. The words are only a memory aid, you would substitute your own words.

Figure 6-7
STRUCTURE FIRST MODEL

ON THE TOPIC . . .

I THINK . . .

BECAUSE . . .

THANK YOU . . .

For the phrase "On the topic" you could say: "I believe there is a problem." "I have a suggestion." "How about this idea?" "Have you considered...." etc.

The phrases "I think" and "Because" could be replaced with: "It seems to me the problem is ... and the solution is ...." "Let's ask, what ...? and I think that the answer is ...." "The other day I was talking to ... and ...." "My experience is that ...." etc.

For the phrase "Thank you" you could substitute: "I hope you'll agree...." "This would be more practical." "I believe this is the main concern." "We all want to see...." "Therefore, I move that...." "Does that answer your question?" etc.

Information first. You also could think of the task as a process. Let's say you've thought of a statement you could make. Keep adding improvements up until the moment you have to speak. Take advantage of all the time you have to develop your one idea.

Figure 6-8
INFORMATION FIRST MODEL

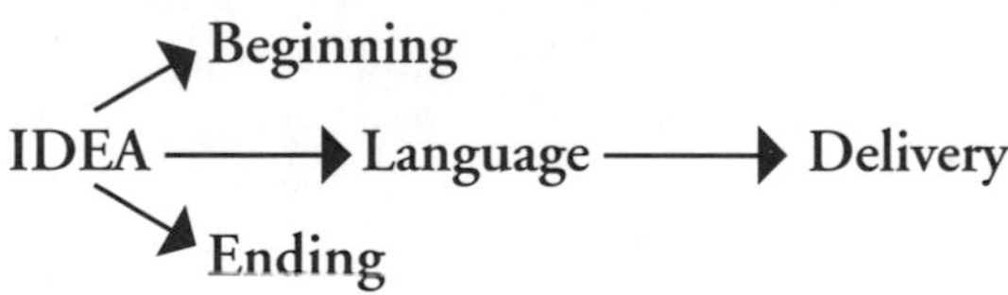

Idea. You could just stand up and say, "I think...." state your thought, that would do the job. But you could make a more impressive presentation if you have time to develop it more...

You could add a *beginning* statement. "Concerning your idea...." "The issue before us...." "I would like to address the problem...." etc. And if you have a little more time to think...

You could add an *ending* statement. "So my suggestion is that we...." "I think that is the best we can say at this time." "What do you think of my idea?" etc. And if you have some more time...

You might think of *language* choices that would add more clarity or force...

You might have time to consider where you could add emphasis to your *delivery.*

Note that you have not added any more ideas, only given structure and clarity to your one thought.

Part II, Chapter 7

Aiding Memory

Personal effectiveness decisions

- I remember ideas better in words. (47%)
- I remember ideas better with pictures in my mind. (39%)
- Equal. (14%)

- It's easier to remember my speech if I break it down into parts. (60%)
- It's easier to remember my speech if I have a general overview. (40%)

- I see the ideas in my speech all connected to each other like a string. (49%)
- I see the ideas in my speech like separate chunks which can be moved around. (35%)
- Both/Other. (16%)

- When rehearsing, I'm silent and don't move. (19%)
- When rehearsing, I speak out loud and move around. (69%)
- I don't rehearse my speeches. (12%)

- The more times I rehearse the more confident I feel. (39%)
- I rehearse just enough for familiarity, but not too much. (51%)
- I don't rehearse my speeches. (10%)

- I do better with my speech written out. (16%)

- I do better with a few notes. (62%)
- I do better with no notes. (22%)

Myth of rote rehearsal

This myth is that many rote repetitions make it easier to remember a speech. The alternative is combining ideas with imagery in a context.

How do you combine ideas with imagery in a context?

The context is the organization of your ideas. Matching ideas to imagery should have been done in the organization stage – now you'll benefit from that pattern. This combination not only helps the audience remember your speech, but it also helps you remember your speech.

Figure 7-1

IDEAS PLUS IMAGERY IN A CONTEXT

Ideas	Context	Imagery
(Abstract)	(Organization)	(Concrete)

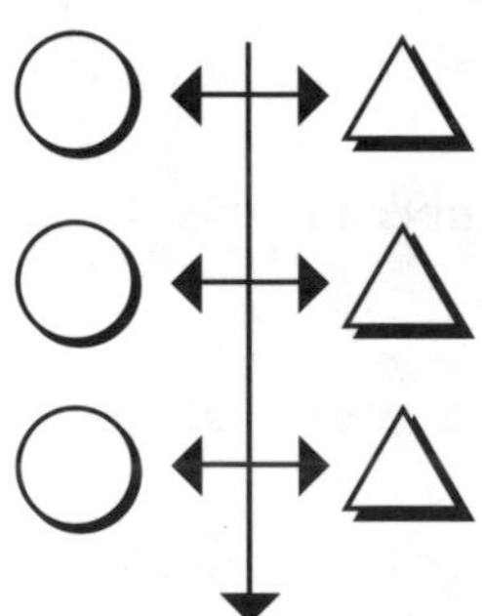

What's the best way to view a speech for purposes of memory?

Think of your speech as having a backbone.

It may be easier to see your speech as consisting primarily of a series of ideas with some added imagery for clarification.

Or, it may be easier to think of our speech as a series of imagery. Each image allows you to suggest an idea for the audience to remember.

Figure 7-2
TWO MEMORY PATTERNS

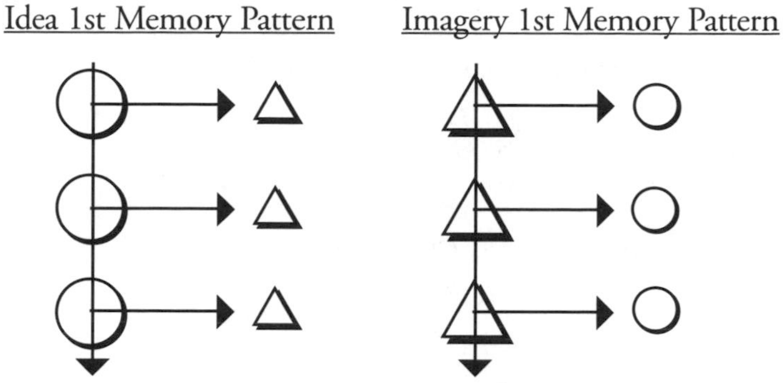

<u>Idea 1st Memory Pattern</u> <u>Imagery 1st Memory Pattern</u>

What types of memory aid can I use?

Memory is facilitated by: 1) delivery notes, 2) visual aid(s), and 3) mental pictures content rehearsal.

Delivery notes. Translate the preparation outline (logical or idea-imagery) that you used for organizing, into delivery notes.

Write down all that you need to have on paper or note cards.

Don't write down any more than you actually need.

You can use sentences, phrases, or single words.

Write out the introduction, and conclusion word-for-word.

Eliminate any outline symbols.

Eliminate less important words.

Write twice as large as normal and double space.

Place the main core of your speech (either ideas or imagery) at the left margin.

Indent the complementary information (either ideas or imagery).

Table 7-1

EXAMPLE OF IDEA 1ST DELIVERY NOTES

THE AGE OF FUTURE SHOCK IS UPON US

WE ARE ALL SUBJECTED TO INSTANT TRAVEL, INSTANT CHANGE AND INSTANT COMMUNICATION.

....

GOVERNMENT, POLITICAL, FAMILIES, BUSINESS

MAN TO MOON

TELEPHONE

SATELLITE, FUNERAL, SPACESHIP, WAR

TECHNICAL-INTERPERS.

INVERSE

ORGAN. MEN

90% ORG.

etc.

Table 7-2

EXAMPLE OF IMAGERY 1ST DELIVERY NOTES

THE AGE OF FUTURE SHOCK IS UPON US

WE ARE ALL SUBJECTED TO INSTANT TRAVEL, INSTANT CHANGE AND INSTANT COMMUNICATION.

....

MAN TO MOON

TELEPHONE

SATELLITE, FUNERAL, SPACESHIP, WAR

GOVERNMENT, POLITICAL, FAMILIES, BUSINESS

TECHNICAL-INTERPERS.

INVERSE

ORGAN. MEN

90% ORG.

etc.

This style of delivery notes facilitates making decisions about what you want to emphasize and what will have less emphasis.

Any idea or imagery could be on the left margin, any idea or imagery could be indented.

Visual aid(s). You could convert your preparation outline into a visual aid or several visual aids. (poster board, flip chart, overhead transparancy, slide, etc.) A visual aid(s) should be:

Well done so it does not become a distraction,
Large enough to be easily seen by everyone,
Placed where everyone can see it,
Revealed only when discussed, then covered up or removed,
Clearly explained,
Smoothly integrated into your speech.

If your visual aid is on a poster board you also can write your notes on the back. Then you can hold it in front of you and read off the back, while maintaining eye contact with the audience. If you use a flip chart, you could write lightly in pencil what you later will write with a bold marker.

Mental pictures content rehearsal. For each main point of your speech create a mental picture that represents that point.

Mentally, place the pictures on the walls of the room around you – one picture on each of the four walls. You can use the ceiling and floor also, if necessary.

When speaking, glance around the room at the walls, remember the pictures, and explain the points. It's better to glance at the walls than down at notes on the lectern.

Figure 7-3
MENTAL PICTURES

Why should I use a language rehearsal?

The more you rehearse, the less you'll need to look at delivery notes.

What's the best way to rehearse language?

Each time you go through your speech, change your words. Don't say an idea the same way twice.

It helps you improve the language in your speech.

It gives you options if you forget something during delivery.

Why should I rehearse delivery?

You feel more free to experiment during rehearsal than during delivery.

Rehearsal is the time when you make the greatest improvement in your delivery.

What's the best way to rehearse delivery?

Stand up, walk, and speak out loud.

Exaggerate your movement, gesture and voice.

Vary your delivery with every repetition of the speech.

Time yourself.

Part II, Chapter 8

Lowering Stress

Personal effectiveness decisions

- When speaking, I tend to freeze up. (24%)
- When speaking, I tend to fidget. (57%)
- Neither. (19%)

- My speech stress consists of a rapid heartbeat. (41%)
- My speech stress consists of sensations in my stomach. (11%)
- I have both rapid heartbeat and sensations in my stomach. (27%)
- I don't have much speech stress. (21%)

- When speaking, I feel my skin getting warm. (66%)
- When speaking, I feel my skin getting cold. (15%)
- Neither. (19%)

- When speaking, my mouth tends to get dry. (58%)
- When speaking, my mouth tends to get moist. (11%)
- Neither. (31%)

- My strength is more in my content. (Ideas, Organization, Language) (49%)
- My strength is more in my delivery. (Movement, Gesture, Voice) (28%)
- My content strength and delivery strength are about equal. (23%)

- My stress decreases after the first few sentences of my speech. (43%)
- My stress decreases sometime during the speech. (32%).
- My stress continues until the speech is over. (25%)

Myth of stage-fright

This myth is that the fight-flight response is the cause of symptoms felt by a speaker. The alternative is speech stress.

What can I expect?

Your symptoms will not be the same as every other speaker.

You'll need to identify your particular symptoms.

You'll need to identify what coping techniques work best for you.

What's the nature of stress?

In a new situation your body creates the potential for two opposite responses: inhibit action, or take action.

The stress response allows you to choose the appropriate balance between the two tendencies in order to create a new skill or behavior pattern.

Figure 8-1
SPEECH STRESS PATTERN

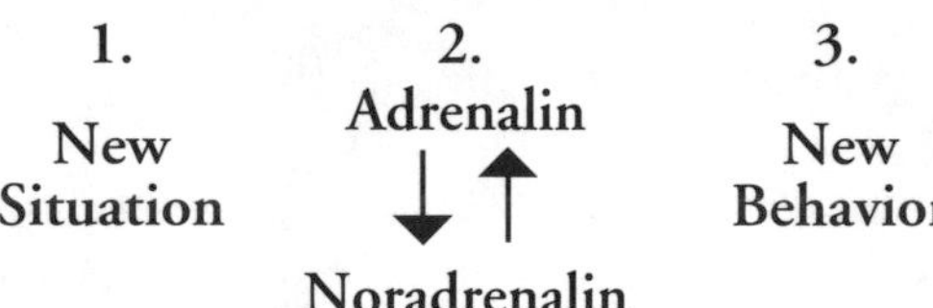

Speech stress is not a negative fear response, but a positive response to new expectations.

How do I prepare mentally?

Make a decision about your state of preparation. Answer the questions below.

Table 8-1
READINESS INVENTORY

Decisions	Circle one		
I think my:	*Weak*	*Average*	*Good*
Subject choice is	-	0	+
Ideas are	-	0	+
Imagery is	-	0	+
Speech nucleus is	-	0	+
Introduction is	-	0	+
Idea-imagery organization is	-	0	+
Conclusion is	-	0	+
Language choices are	-	0	+
Delivery plan is	-	0	+
Rehearsals have been	-	0	+
Totals:	___	___	___

If there are more plus responses than minus responses, you are ready to speak.

How do I prepare emotionally?

Plan beforehand how you are going to react when you begin to experience stress.

Analytical thinking tends to replace emotional thinking, therefore objectively observe your symptoms, interpret them positively, and evaluate them positively.

Objective observation
Analyze symptoms,
Recognize that your symptoms are unique to you,
Note exactly where they are and when they occurred in your body,
Note exactly when they increased or decreased,
Note how severe they really are, be objective.

Positive interpretation
Recognize how you can capitalize on the energy increase.

Positive evaluation
Remember positive aspects of previous speeches.
Remember the decrease in symptoms in previous speeches.

How do I prepare physically?

Tense and relax the major muscle groups in your body, then visualize yourself speaking without tension in your body.

Relaxation is facilitated by first tensing a muscle. Follow these steps:

Find a place where you will not be disturbed,

Sit in a comfortable chair that gives support to your head and arms, put both feet flat on the floor,

Close your eyes, take a couple of deep breaths and let the air out slowly,

Tense your right fist and arm for approximately five seconds and then let your arm drop and feel the relaxation of the muscles,

Tense the muscles of your left fist and arm (five seconds) and let them relax,

Tense the muscles of your face and throat and then relax them,

Tense the muscles of your chest, back and stomach, then relax,

Tense the muscles of your right leg and foot, then relax,

Tense the muscles of your left leg and foot, then relax.

You should be totally relaxed without tension in any muscle of your body.

Visualize. Now you are ready to begin conditioning that relaxed state to the act of delivering your speech.

Construct a series of mental pictures that take you up to the moment of delivery. As an example, here is a series of images for a student in a public speaking class.

0. You are sitting in your room completely relaxed.
1. You are in your room working on your speech.
2. You are in your class, one week before your speech, listening to students speaking.
3. You are in your room, one week before, rehearsing your speech.
4. You are in your room, the day before you speak, rehearsing your speech.
5. You are in your room, the day you will speak, getting ready to go to class.
6. You are walking across campus on your way to class, thinking about your speech.

7. You are walking into your class and taking your seat.
8. You are listening to other speakers.
9. Your name is called and you walk up to the front of the room.
10. You give your speech.

The basic procedure is to begin by relaxing fully, as described above, and then picture in your mind the zero state or mental picture that should arouse no tension at all.

Then you visualize the first image and mentally check the major muscle groups of your body to see if any tension occurs. If tension is present then you immediately stop the visualization and return to the relaxed state.

After you have remained relaxed for a few seconds you repeat the first picture again and hold it to see if any tension occurs.

If this time you do not detect any tension in your muscles then you move on to picture the second image and note if any tension arises. Any time tension is felt you stop the visualization and return to the completely relaxed state.

You may only be able to progress to the second or third picture in your first session, but each time you practice, you begin at zero and see how far you can go without arousing any tension.

When you are able to picture yourself speaking to your audience without feeling any muscular tension you will have the maximum carry-over into your actual delivery.

You will feel much less tension than you otherwise would have when speaking. The more practice, naturally, the better the results.

Why do I forget things when I stand up to speak?

Increase of physiological arousal can interfere with memory. Something you learn at one level of arousal will be best remembered at that same level of arousal.

If your rehearsal was at a very low level and your delivery is at a high level (typical) you may have trouble remembering.

The best strategy is to increase your energy level during rehearsal so it will be closer to the level of arousal in the speaking situation.

Part II, Chapter 9

Speaking

Personal effectiveness decisions

- Just before speaking, I review my speech. (68%)
- Just before speaking, I try not to think about my speech. (32%)

- Before speaking, I talk to myself in a positive way. (17%)
- Before speaking, I visualize myself speaking well. (35%)
- Before speaking, I tense and relax my muscles. (14%)
- None of the above. (34%)

- My delivery tends to be low energy. (10%)
- My delivery tends to be high energy. (44%)
- My delivery energy level is about average. (46%)

- My delivery is the same regardless of speech purpose. (41%)
- I change my delivery depending on the speech purpose. (59%)

- I have some awareness of the audience when I speak. (54%)
- I'm highly aware of the audience when I speak. (46%)

- I don't vary my speech in response to audience feedback. (47%)
- I change my organization, language, or delivery in response to audience feedback. (53%)

- When speaking, I tend to shorten my speech. (31%)
- When speaking, I tend to expand on my speech. (33%)
- I keep my speech as planned. (36%)

Myth of passive delivery

This myth is that a speaker should not move or gesture. The alternative is audience adaptation.

How can I reduce stress immediately prior to speaking?

Repeat briefly, the three types of rehearsal techniques.

Mental coping.

Remind yourself that you are "ready."

Review your speech if it helps. Go over your beginning, ideas, language, delivery,

Emotional coping.

Interpret any symptoms in your body as a sign you will do well.

Use positive self-talk. Encourage yourself.

Physical coping.

Take slow, deep breaths.

Unobtrusively, tense and relax your muscles.

Should I imagine the audience in an embarrasing situation?

No. Creating an embarrasing picture of them would be a distraction for you.

Most people in an audience don't have strong feelings either for or against you. The most common problem is apathy.

Is there anything I can do during delivery to relieve stress?

Yes, be proactive.

Unobtrusively take a deep breath.

Speak with more energy, project your voice.

Move and gesture.

How do I use delivery notes?

Get them out of your hands. Place them on the lectern and don't touch them.

If you have more than one page or card, slide the top one off to the side.

Don't turn it over or place it behind the others – that distracts.

Does the speech purpose affect my delivery?

Yes. Create a mind-set or attitude toward your audience.

With the awareness speech, you inspire like a minister.
With the information speech, you lecture like a teacher.
With the argument speech, you advocate like a lawyer.
With the action speech, you motivate like a salesperson.

Do I really need to use gestures?

Yes. Gestures, and also taking a step or two, have real benefits. They:

Regain attention that you will lose periodically,
Build trust, when consistent with your words.
Clarify your meaning,
Indicate which points are most important to remember.

How do I improve my delivery?

Follow your delivery plan.

A delivery plan eliminates boring delivery for the low energy speaker.

A delivery plan eliminates distracting behavior for the high energy speaker.

You could mark a word or phrase you want to emphasize.

You could mark where you will show a visual aid.

I don't notice much audience feedback, why is that?

When you are more confident about remembering your speech you can direct more attention to your delivery and to your audience.

As appropriate movement and gestures are mastered, they require less attention.

As appropriate variety in vocal patterns is mastered, it requires less attention.

As your language skills increase, they require less attention.

With more attention freed up, you can pay more attention to reading audience feedback and adapting to it.

Figure 9-1
SPEAKER'S ATTENTION

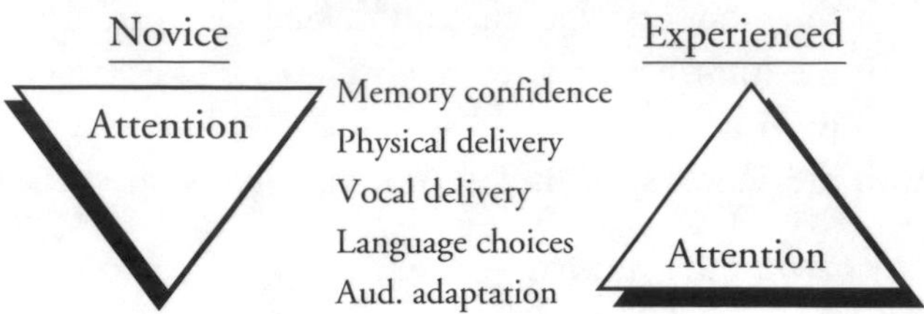

How can I learn to look at the audience?

To begin, just look at one person.

Then, look at only friendly faces.

Then, look at more people, and eventually everyone.

How do I adapt to an audience?

You decide whether the audience response is mostly positive or mostly negative.

Positive feedback is eye-contact, smiles, and nods.

Negative feedback is no eye-contact, frowns, or shaking heads.

Then, follow the audience adaptation formula.

If the feedback is largely positive, you continue with your speech as planned.

If the feedback is largely negative, you need to make a change.

Figure 9-2
AUDIENCE ADAPTATION

Feedback		Speaker
Positive	→	**Continue**
Negative	→	**Change**

What kind of adaptation can I make?

Easiest to change is delivery – physical movement, more emphatic gesture, or vocal expressiveness.

Next easiest to change is to use more emphatic language.

You can skip ahead to more interesting content.

You may add some imagery material that you had previously deleted during your speech preparation.

How do I evaluate myself after the speech?

Use this form as soon after speaking as practical to review your speech. You want to derive as much learning as possible for the next time you speak.

Figure 9-3
SELF EVALUATION

Posture/Move.	Unaware ( )	Aware ( )		Made changes ( )
Gesture	Unaware ( )	Aware ( )		Made changes ( )
Eye-contact	Unaware ( )	Aware ( )		Made changes ( )
Voice	Unaware ( )	Aware ( )		Made changes ( )
Memory	Problem obvious ( )	Covered up ( )		No problem ( )
Aud. response	Unaware ( )	Negative ( )	Mixed ( )	Positive ( )
Content plan	No change ( )	Deleted material ( )		Elaborated ( )
Language plan	Unaware ( )	Aware ( )		Made changes ( )
Delivery plan	No change ( )	Less emphasis ( )		More emphasis ( )
Speech length	Unaware ( )	Slower than rehearsal ( )		Faster ( )
Speech stress	Increased ( )	Decreased at end ( )		
	Decreased in middle ( )	Decreased after beginning ( )		

Anything go wrong?______________________________

Anything go especially well? __________________________

Changes to make in preparation next time: __________________

Changes to make in delivery next time: ____________________

What kind of speech assessment do I need from my audience?

The Speech Progress Chart portrays speaking skills graphically on a scale from ineffective to effective.

Figure 9-4
SPEECH PROGRESS CHART

Beginning Weak__________ Average__________ Good__________ Strong
Weak means difficult to hear. Strong means emphasis.

Movement Random/lean ______ Poised__________ Pacing ________ Varied
Radom is distracting foot movements or swaying. Lean is standing with the weight on one foot. Poised means good posture. Pacing means repetitious walking, varied means taking steps has variety.

Gesture
Few __________ Many
Random__________ None ______ Weak __________ Strong
Repetitious __________ Varied
Random hand movements, like fingering note cards or rubbing hands, are distracting. Gestures should be appropriate to the size of the audience, but generally, many gestures are preferred to a few, strong ones are better than weak and varied are better than repetitious.

Distraction Physical ______________________________
Physical distractions include things like: a pen in the hand, tapping fingers, playing with a ring or hair, etc.

Eye-contact Little ________ Half time__________ Good ________ Continual
Little eye-contact is looking down or looking above the heads of the audience. Continual means direct eye-contact with individuals, including virtually everyone.

Loudness Weak________ Average __________ Good ________ Projection
A weak voice forces the audience to strain to hear. Projection makes listening comfortable.

Sounds Read __________ Average__________ Well
______ First time
Memorized ________ Average__________ Well
Regardless of whether the speech is given with or without notes, or is read – how does it sound? Some people read poorly and some read well. A memorized speech may sound mechanical or sound good. Ideally a speech should sound like it is being said for the "first time."

Pace Rushed __________ Fast
Hesitations ________ Jerky__________ Good ________ Varied
Drags __________ Slow
The rate of speaking should neither be rushed nor drag. Dysfluencies, awkward pauses or hesitations in speaking are also very distracting. Conversational speaking has variety in rate and natural pauses.

Distraction — Vocal ______________________________

Vocal would include words or sounds used excessively, like: "um," "ah," "OK," "you know."

Ending — Weak__________ Average________ Good_______Strong

The ending should be as strong as the beginning, or stronger.

Time — Over __________________ / Under __________________ | ____________Well timed

Some audience members may quit listening if the speech goes too long. But, if the speech is too short the audience may feel short-changed.

Intro. (why) — Negative _________ Abrupt ________ Good ______Relevant

Making apologies is a negative beginning. The beginning answers the question, "Why should the audience listen?"

Preview (what) — None__________ Brief________ | Ideas________Prominent / Purpose _____Prominent

A preview answers the question, "what" the speech is about. A brief statement is OK, but a stronger statement reveals the ideas or purpose of the speech. It is sometimes called the thesis or speech goal.

Form — Written ________ Average_______ Good______Conversational

The written form has long sentences composed of several clauses/phrases (subordination) and a varied vocabulary. The speaking idiom is conversational and consists of short, simple sentences and short, familiar words. Ideas are related by simple juxtaposition (two ideas next to each other), a lot of repetition, active voice, and personal references: *I, you, we, us,* etc.

Language — Vague/slang ____ Average ____ | Good Explanation _____ Precise / Good Description ______ Vivid

Vague language is very general, slang is an example. Explanation, which often dominates in information and argument speeches, should be precise. Description, which may dominate in awareness and action speeches, should be vivid.

Transitions — None_________ Brief_________ Good_________Prominent

Content taken verbatim from written material often has no transitions. Brief means a single word or short phrase: *first, second, on the other hand, in contrast,* etc. Prominent means at least a complete sentence to indicate the change from one point to another. Listeners should be able to identify the organizational structure of the speech: chronological, cause-effect, problem-solution, etc.

Source

None cited__________ Personal _______Good _____Expert
None cited__________ Popular ________ Good ___Authority

A speaker should reveal the source of his or her information. This is critical to an ethical message and makes the speaker more credible. Sometimes the speaker is an expert in the subject. A popular magazine or book is OK, but information from an authoritative source is best.

Purpose

Weak awareness ___ Average _______ Good _____ New priority
The focus of the awareness speech (special occasion) is on priorities. The content is primarily values. “What is important?” The structure is comparing.

Weak information __ Average _______ Good_______ New belief
The focus of the information speech is on beliefs. The content is primarily concepts. “What is it?” The structure is clarifying.

Weak argument ____ Average _______ Good_____ New attitude
The focus of the argument speech is on attitudes. The content is primarily evidence. “What is best?” The structure is reasoning.

Weak action_______ Average _______ Good ____ New behavior
The focus of the action speech is on behaviors. The content is primarily illustrations. “What should I do?” The structure is motivating.

Review (what)

None __________ Brief ______ Idea summary _____Prominent
None __________ Brief ______ Purpose summary___Prominent

The review summarizes what was in the speech. It is similar to the preview.

Conc. (why)

Negative __________ Abrupt _________ Good ______Relevant
The conclusion gives closure to the message and often that is done by referring back to the beginning. A negative note can undermine the entire speech. The conclusion answers the question, “Why should the audience remember the speech?”

Of the four purpose patterns (Awareness, Information, Argument, Action), normally only one is used for a given speech. However, a longer speech could have more than one purpose.

Delivery and content are given equal importance. Delivery variables are grouped on the left side of the form and content variables are on the right side.

The arrangement of speaking variables facilitates checking behavioral descriptions during the speech. The rater can start at the top of the chart as the speaker begins and proceed to the bottom as the speech progresses, so that the evaluation will be completed when the speech ends.

Assessments can be made with an "x," or circle on each line.

If a change occurs during the speech (for example, a weak voice becomes stronger) a new mark may be made and an arrow drawn to indicate the direction of the change.

When the speech is over, look at all the delivery variables on the left side and give a summary evaluation on the line at the bottom of the chart.

Then do the same thing for the content variables on the right side. The final evaluation, would be an average.

Part III, Chapter 10

A Professional Approach

Myth of rhetoric. While some rhetorical concepts are still valuable today, much about purposes, organization, language, and delivery style is not.

Society is different. Modern societies have less rigidly defined social roles than in the past. Greece, for example, was a slave state. Class duties and privileges were clearly defined and enforced. Now, cultures are more complex, pluralistic and diversified.

Audiences are different. Anciently, public speaking was exclusively the province of the courts, the legislative forum, and ceremonial occasions. Now it pervades all areas of life: business, education, politics, religion, etc.

Technology is different. Technology has both increased the reach of the speaker and increased audience expectations. A speech may be heard around the world, but the speech which lasted an hour or more is being replaced by the fifteen minute speech which still may seem too long for some people.

Speaker-listener roles are different. There is a new awareness that the power of the speaker is more than matched by the power of the listener. A speaker dominated model of communication is no longer accepted. One scholar bluntly concludes, "...message-driven conceptions just don't work."[1]

The concept of a message is different. There has also been a shift from the Aristotelian view that all speaking is persuasion to the concept of information processing, that information is neutral and can be understood or interpreted in various ways, only one of which is persuasion.

> The tradition of definition which has forwarded an exclusionary view of rhetoric as persuasion, communication as influence, and discourse as social power has negated an equally compelling view of communication as relational responsibility. Communication is fundamentally concerned with both influence and relationships. As such, it expresses both our individual autonomy and mutual responsibility.[2]

The concept of language is different. Originally, there was little difference between speaking and writing. Books were written versions of speeches, dialogues, or monologues. Figures of speech became literary devices. But gradually, the written word evolved into specialized forms. Now the structure and function of spoken and written language have become virtually opposite to each other.

The concept of thinking is different. For a long time it was assumed that there was one correct way to think. Logic was taught as the way to discover truth. Then, the scientific process of discovery became the model. Later, the process of creative thinking was studied. But now, we're aware of different thinking styles and different learning styles and even different types of intelligence.

In brief, while still other changes could be mentioned, these alone demand fundamental changes in the art and science of public speaking. The alternative to the myth of rhetoric is modern social science.

Social science. A professional seeks out the best information available. New discoveries about the nature of reality and the nature of human beings all affect the nature of communication.

> Intentionally or not, we work from a world view that has been derived from the natural sciences. But the science has changed. If we are to continue to draw from the sciences to create and manage organizations, to design research, and to formulate hypotheses about organizational design, planning, economics, human nature, and change processes (the list can be much longer), then we need to at least ground our work in the science of our times. We need to stop seeking after the universe of the seventeenth century and begin to explore what has become known to us in the twentieth century.[3]

Science is a process of continual discovery and there is always something more to learn about the craft of speaking.

Personal effectiveness. Vilfredo Pareto discovered the principle of effectiveness in human behavior which is commonly referred to as the 80-20 principle. Generally, 80 percent of your effectiveness results from 20 percent of what you do. For example, 80 percent of music sales are from about 20 percent of all recording artists. Eighty percent of the productivity of most organizations come from 20 percent of it's people. Eighty percent of the profit may come from 20 percent of the complete line of products, etc.

This is not a precise ratio, it could in some instances be 70-30 or even 90-10, but there is not a one-to-one relationship between actions and the degree of success you achieve.

The ratio operates in analyzing negative effects as well. In an organization it is not uncommon that 80 percent of the problems come from only 20 percent of the people. And 80 percent of the flaws in a production run may come from only 20 percent of the different operations.

The point is, some things you do are much more important than others. This book does not try to cover all that could be said about public speaking – it attempts to identify critical tasks which make the most difference.

Personal strengths. The more responsibility you take for learning the faster you learn. And one of the first things you discover is that you have a personal learning style. For each individual, some ways are easier while others require much more effort. So you need to identify your strengths to make your learning more effective.

As individuals develop their speaking styles – conformity decreases, originality increases. The most critical difference for a speaker is how he or she plans, creates, organizes, remembers, and speaks.

Personal ethics. Simplified, ethics is an honest relationship between you and your audience. You and your audience should have equal freedom to choose in your relationship. That freedom rests on a foundation of respect.

> Rhetoric requires that audiences be free to choose to agree or disagree with the writer or speaker, to choose to persuade or not to persuade themselves.[4]

> Honesty, in the sense of self-confrontation and self-revelation, is for me the prime rhetorical good.[5]

> As a rhetorician you function within an eternal dialectic: on the one hand, you attempt to persuade an audience; on the other, you demand that that audience choose freely for itself.
>
> Rhetorical discourses, at their best, are exciting just because the speaker or writer believes as strongly as he does and still leaves his audience free to choose their beliefs. The great rhetorician keeps no secrets: he admits his own biases and his desire that the audience share them, and at the same time he insists that the audience make their own choices.[6]

The prime force that drives the speech cycle is the speaker-audience relationship. And since every relationship has an ethical dimension, it should be obvious that powerful speaking proceeds from authentic relationships. The basic motivation to give a speech is not for the speaker's benefit, but to help members of an audience make better decisions. It is the stance of the servant-leader.

Therefore, ethical considerations are an integral part of the entire speech preparation and delivery cycle from beginning to end. Here are some examples:

1) Getting subjects. You show equal respect for people who disagree with you, as you do for those who agree with you.
2) Organizing plans. You don't hesitate to reveal your relevant personal values, beliefs, attitudes, and behaviors to your audience.
3) Aiding memory. Accompanying your ideas, you always cite your source of information.
4) Lowering stress. You don't pretend to be someone you're not – no tricks, gimmicks or games.
5) Speaking. You adapt your message and delivery in response to audience feedback. Their understanding is more important than your "speech."

Ethics arise naturally from the character of the speaker and culminate in effective communication. The reason for honesty is to create an authentic relationship which is its own justification. However, there are also by-products of an authentic relationship, among which are: 1) increased confidence in your verbal-nonverbal consistency, 2) increased confidence in overcoming speech stress, and 3) increased confidence in the impact of your message.

Note the words of Aleksander Solzhenitsyn in his Nobel Prize acceptance speech.

> ...a work of art bears within itself its own confirmation: concepts which are manufactured out of whole cloth or overstrained will not stand up to being tested in images, will somehow fall apart and turn out to be sickly pallid and convincing to no one. Works steeped in truth and presented to us vividly alive take hold of us, will attract us to themselves with great power – and no one, ever, even in a later age, will presume to negate them.[7]

You begin with statements which you believe are accurate and will help others, then you plan the organization, adapt the language, and consider the manner of presentation to make them crystal clear. That is very different from starting with what people want to hear and telling it to them so you can achieve influence for your own benefit.

Professionals know the power of honesty. Following is a excerpt from the National Speakers Association Code of Professional Ethics.

> I pledge myself to honesty and integrity; to pursue my profession and education to the end that service to my clients shall always be maintained at the highest possible level.[8]

An audience grants you time, attention, and access to their thoughts which leaves them somewhat vulnerable. The unstated contract of trust is that whatever you say will be the truth as well as you know it and you will not exploit their weakness or ignorance. They would not listen to you for a minute if they thought you would deceive them. Communication exists on the assumption of trust and you violate it at great risk.

Personal speech cycle decisions. The speech cycle outlines the types of decisions which you make as you prepare a speech. The first letter of the separate parts: Getting subjects, Organizing plans, Aiding memory, Lowering stress, Speaking, produces the acronym GOALS, reminding you that the entire process is goal-oriented. You expect to achieve the goals that you select, and your audience expects to achieve their goals. When the two sets of goals coincide and are achieved, your success becomes their success.

Getting subjects begins with the last speech you gave. Think back to the last time you spoke and remember what was successful. Then get a clear image of the new audience in your mind because that mental picture will influence all the decisions you make. From the comparison of that image with your self-image will flow all other decisions. To select material – use your personal expertise, and you may use creative techniques to spark your imagination, and you may want to search other resources, like a library.

As you move into the phase of *organizing,* you'll make decisions about the content, the language relationships, and your delivery. Some material may be discarded and you may have to search for new material.

In the *aiding memory* phase you create memory bonds between the different parts of your speech. A memory link is forged by different types of rehearsals: a content rehearsal, a language rehearsal, and a delivery rehearsal.

Lowering stress is the next phase. You review your preparation and make a decision about your state of readiness. You also can practice positive self-talk to prepare emotionally, and desensitization is an effective physical preparation.

Then, when you are in the actual situation you can use specific coping techniques: review your delivery plan, positively interpret your arousal level, and release your tension.

The culmination of all your work is *speaking.* At its best, it is a dynamic interaction between you and your audience. The most powerful "teacher" of public speaking is the audience. It is their feedback which tells you how well you are communicating. Learning how to observe the audience and how to adapt to feedback is the heart and soul of speaking.

This model is only sequential in the passage of time as you make each decision, but it's a complex system wherein each decision is related to every other one. "Reality is made up of circles but we see straight lines."[9]

Part III, Chapter 11

Live Speaking Situations

Myth of attention factors. Faculty psychology was an early theory which held that people had specific areas in the brain (faculties) which were responsible for specific mental processes, like attention. The factors controlling attention were supposed to be: activity, reality, proximity, familiarity, novelty, suspense, conflict, humor, and vital. The fact of the matter is that no stimulus has one consistent response.

> ...sociocentric notions about a world filled with objectively pleasant stimuli seem biologically indefensible....[1]

An alternative to the attention factors is to understand the psychological constraints in a live speaking situation: attention, perception, language, and memory.

Attention. *Conversational limit.* Under typical circumstances, conversations have a four-minute barrier. Whether speaking to a stranger, or a friend, on average, people take about four minutes to decide whether they want to break off that contact or will continue to talk.[2] The listener to a speech is likely to make a decision to discontinue listening in much less time. So the range of time that you could expect normal attention or interest is usually only a few minutes. Therefore your message must have high relevance to the audience.

Sustained attention limit. Our senses have limits to how much information can be seen or heard and how quickly the information can be dealt with; we can only understand so much, so fast. Some researchers say that short term memory is 60 seconds.[3] Others state that short term memory is 10 to 30 seconds, but it depends on the nature of the task.[4] An average estimate would be about 40 seconds. In any case, it is extremely brief and you have to show something original about that information if you want it to be considered for a longer time – moved to long term memory.

> There is no such thing as voluntary attention sustained for more than a few seconds at a time. What is called sustained voluntary attention is a repetition of successive efforts which bring back the topic to mind.[5]

Thus the speaking situation is characterized by decreasing attention. Throughout your speech you have to continually re-capture it. And that is done with relevance, originality, and especially, change.

> We don't perceive the world as it is, because our nervous system evolved to select only a small extract of reality and to ignore the rest. ... Instead of conveying everything about the world, our nervous system is "impressed" only by *dramatic changes.*[6]

Perception. Research on the perception of speakers shows that credibility is the most important variable.

> ...one may...say that with some frequency two very broad (and sensible) dimensions have in fact commonly emerged in factor-analytic investigations of communicator credibility. These are variously labeled in the literature, but two useful terms are "competence" and "trustworthiness."[7]

> Perhaps it is not surprising that both competence and trustworthiness emerge as basic dimensions of credibility, since as a rule only the conjunction of competence and trustworthiness make for reliable communications.[8]

Credibility is also related to a lesser degree to other factors like: dynamism, liking, fluency, sources, etc. but those factors vary depending on the audience, situation, and message.[9] In factor analysis research, usually the first two variables account for the majority of the concept being investigated and that's what the 80-20 principle is all about. Dynamism has already been discussed as the need to continually recapture the interest of the audience, and the other factors will be dealt with in other contexts.

Expertise. The keys to expertise (competence) are experience and authoritative sources. The audience expects you to have some first-hand knowledge of the subject you are addressing or to have researched the subject carefully. But if you don't reveal your experience, or cite your sources – there is no presumption of expertise.

Trust. The keys to trust are self-disclosure and nonverbal consistency. In the words of Campbell,

> ...the writer or speaker who behaves rhetorically presents himself to his audience. He stands before them figuratively or physically, wearing no mask, hiding behind no facade. ... The furthest extreme from Rhetoric is the performer who spends his life reading Hamlet's lines, or Lear's, or Othello's, and who may never disclose himself to his audience in any meaningful fashion. ... The rhetorician, on the other hand, is constantly disclosing himself to his audience. We say, almost instinctively, that the rhetorician who hides behind words, behind platitudes, behind the easy, glib phrase is unreal, a phony.[10]

> ...you function best, you help your audience to achieve the highest level of consciously exercised free choice by the honesty of self-confrontation and self-exposure.[11]

Perception pyramid. Research by Merhabian and Wiener[12] shows that when there is ambiguity in a communication, the nonverbal cues will be given more weight in deciding on the attitude toward the speaker. The reaction to a speaker in an ambiguous situation has been estimated to consist of a physical dimension which constitutes 55% of the total impact, the voice which contributes another 38% and language which adds the additional 7%. While those figures are only rough estimates, the point is there is a significant difference in impact by the different aspects of a communication.

Another researcher believes that 70% should be attributed to the visual dimension.[13] Thus, physical and vocal cues are used to reduce ambiguity. They can add clarity and reinforce meaning. But, that also means they can be equally powerful distractions.

Language. Oral communication requires instant comprehension. Writing and speaking are each a complete system of meaning with different structural patterns. Some people are much better at speaking, others are superior in writing.

There are of course similarities in the two systems, but "Just write the way you talk," is very poor advice to give a writer and "Just speak the way you think," is equally poor advice for a public speaker.

> Most people...maintain quite a disparity between the language they speak (to friends, acquaintances), the language they read (newspapers, magazines, biographies, detective stories, novels, histories), and the language they write (bills, memos, reports, letters). Homogeneity of language would be tedious and ineffective; this diversity of spoken and written language permits a range of communication.[14]

Reading versus listening. Listening in a public place is psychologically opposite from reading in solitude. The reading situation is usually one in which there are competing messages present; there are other articles in a magazine, other stories in a newspaper, other books to read, etc. The writer has a greater burden in attracting initial interest compared to other written material which is equally available. Thus the writer has to use a provocative title, a first sentence that is intriguing, and a first paragraph that arouses high interest.

Also, you typically read in a quiet place. Therefore, once the reader has begun, external distractions are minimal, or easy to ignore, and interest is more easily maintained because the reader is concentrating on interpreting the meaning of the words.

The speaking situation however, is quite different. There are no other competing speakers. A speaker has a few seconds at the beginning when everyone is curious, so initially you have their undivided attention. But, since there are many distractions in the environment, attention can quickly drift to the surroundings, to other people in the audience, or to random thoughts. The speaker, after the beginning, has to cope with decreasing interest by the listeners.

Thus, the writer has more difficulty in getting initial attention, but maintains it more easily because the act of reading requires more effort. In contrast, a speaker has audience interest initially, but can lose it quickly.

So speakers who believe they must get attention at the beginning, but have no further regard for keeping attention do not understand the speaking environment.

Consider also the ending of a written message and a speech. If the story you are reading becomes uninteresting you could simply stop. If you read to the end and are disappointed, you have only yourself to blame. But there are higher expectations on the part of an audience. If they lose interest in the speech they blame only you.

Because the two situations are opposites there must be significant differences in how each message is organized.

Juxtaposition. One way of generating meaning is to place one idea in a superior position to another. That relationship is called subordination and is more commonly found in writing. Giving equal weight to two ideas is called juxtaposition. And that is the predominant form of spoken discourse.

> ...where the written language makes use of subordination, spoken language makes use of juxtaposition. Being comparatively flexible and nimble, spoken language indicates the bond between the different clauses in the briefest and simplest way.[15]

Subordination makes possible greater complexity.

> As a person's reading vocabulary develops far beyond the vocabulary he uses in casual conversations, so his understanding of the complexities of sentence and paragraph structure usually outstrips the language he speaks.[16]

There is also a great difference in the ability of writing and speaking to reflect subtlety of ideas.

> A writer, ...can indulge in nuances to his heart's content. All he has to do is to set them before his readers: If the readers miss them, they can always reread, turn back to a clause or a paragraph, or perhaps catch them on the third or fourth reading. But in the one-time encounter that is the speech, no such possibility exists. If the nuances, if the subtleties, are lost, the speaker cannot represent them.[17]

Because of writing's greater complexity and subtlety, more ideas can be packed into writing than speaking.

Redundancy. Perhaps you've been told that in writing you should not use an important word more than once, that you should use a synonym or phrase each time you refer to the same concept. In speaking you should always use the same word every time you mention the same idea.

> The spoken language is characterized by greater redundancy. ...in discussing the written language...it is regarded as a fault. In the spoken language, however, it need not be a fault at all but a positive virtue.[18]

> ...the common use – perhaps over-use – of apposition, for purposes of clarifying, explaining, reinforcing. Or the various modes of restatement, recapitulation, repetition, reprise. These practices – which would be impossibly irritating and insufferably patronizing in written prose – are quite naturally and generously utilized by an effective speaker; for he knows it is essential to keep his listeners with him.[19]

The smooth flow of most writing typically puts an audience to sleep. And the dramatic changes in speaking could be disturbing to a reader. Each has a structure suited to the different psychological situations.

Informality. A relationship is powerfully affected by the choice of a formal or a personal language style. Active voice is even more important in speaking than writing. For example, "The weak, the complicated and the long drawn-out are to be avoided." That passive form should be changed to active language, "Choose action words and moving sentences." "Avoid weakness and complexity."

Speaking also has more personal pronouns. It is effective to speak directly to the audience:

Claim mutual concerns by using the words, *we, us.*

Reveal your ideas and feelings by saying, *I....*

Address them personally, *you....*

Vocal pauses are also natural in conversational language.

> These used to be thought faults, and children were often told not to say 'er'. We are now realizing that to 'er' is human. Stabilizers such as this occur particularly when we are thinking aloud, defining more precisely, seeking a vivid expression.... They help the listener also by pacing the ideas and helping him to think with the speaker.[20]

Delivery. Variety is necessary to avoid monotony. Writing achieves variety by sentence structure and vocabularly. Speaking achieves variety by delivery, so a speaker needs to learn an entirely different structure from those taught in English classes and a completely different set of standards for evaluation.

> ...a writer can make far greater demands upon the assimilative powers of a reader's mind than can a speaker upon the assimilative power of a listener's mind.... Both listener and reader must reprocess the verbal symbols that they ingest, but

> the reader is in a mental set for much stouter mental exertion. He is not so relaxed as the listener, who sits back as he watches somebody else do the work. The reader has to do the work for himself.... ...the reader can always return with refreshed attention after a nod. But the speaker, if he detects the signs of flagging attention, must do something remedial at once and with deceptive skill. And if he suddenly decides to telescope three points into one or to jettison several important ideas, he cannot be blamed. For if he doesn't he may end up with even greater intellectual losses than these.[21]

In summary, a live speech has a different language pattern than writing. It is a separate art.

> A good speech should not necessarily read well. It is created for the ear not the eye. It demands instantaneous comprehension.... That is why the art of making a speech is unique. That is why prepared written addresses are almost always bad. They please the eye but the ear's standards are different.[22]

Memory. *Next day.* There are various estimates of the forgetting curve, but all agree the first day has the largest loss – and it is considerably more than half. You can use one-fourth as an average. Therefore, you have to design a message very carefully and deliver it well to be effective.

Number of points. The limits of short term memory are seven, plus or minus two.[23] Thus, five or fewer is about the number of main points that can be easily remembered. But, if there is high interest, more ideas could be remembered.

Position. Meaningful attention is related to a *change* of thought – particularly when something begins or when it ends.

> In psychology experiments, a word at the beginning of a list heard once is recalled 70 percent of the time, words in the middle less than 20 percent, and words at the end almost 100 percent.[24]

Good recall for the beginning is called the primacy effect (the first in a series) and good recall of the ending is called the recency effect (the last in a series).

Recall is also helped by transitional words because they emphasize that new beginning effect. Breaking up information into smaller "chunks" increases the number of new beginnings.

Also, a word that stands out as different from surrounding words grabs attention. Something unexpected or unusual is remembered better, that is called the Von Restorff effect.

Abstract-concrete. The brain hemispheres perceive and store information differently; one brain function stores primarily words and the other function stores primarily pictures.

> ...the contents of concrete sentences are stored primarily as visual images and the contents of abstract sentences primarily verbally.[25]

However, it's desirable to combine both hemisphere functions to maximize recall. This point will be discussed more in chapter 16.

Emotion. Just as you cannot have an emotion without it being related to some idea, you also can't have an idea which is devoid of emotional relationship.

> In fact, it is entirely possible that the very first stage of the organism's reaction to stimuli and the very first elements in retrieval are affective.[26]

Emotions evoke ideas and ideas evoke emotions. The important thing to remember is you can lengthen recall of ideas by relating them to feelings.[27]

The organization of ideas we call chunking is comparable to the pattern of emotion we could call emphasis. Creating smaller chunks improves memory. Creating more frequent change in emotional emphasis improves memory. Memory is improved by organization, and language, and delivery.

Speech format. The realities of attention, perception, language, and memory suggest a structure for a speech consisting of an introduction, preview, message, review, and conclusion. This pattern will be discussed in detail in chapter 15.

Part III, Chapter 12

Audience Decision Making

Myth of need-motivation. Freud introduced the idea that drives and needs determine behavior. That idea has had a powerful influence and its most practical application is by Maslow who suggests that needs may be arranged in an hierarchy to explain motivation. But even he realized the limitation of relying on needs to explain behavior.

> Not all behavior is determined by the basic needs. We might even say that not all behavior is motivated. There are many determinants of behavior other than motives.[1]

More importantly, he said his theory had relevance only briefly, in cases of threat.

> The perfectly healthy, normal, fortunate man has no sex needs or hunger needs, or needs for safety, or for love, or for prestige, or self-esteem, except in stray moments of quickly passing threat.[2]

In confirmation, researchers have not found much relationship between need satisfaction and motivation.

> Maslow's theory continues to be featured in motivational textbooks and seminars, even though there is little empirical support for the assumption that needs are hierarchically organized and inadequate of conceptual clarity with regard to the content of the higher-order needs in his taxonomy.[3]

> ...the Maslow model is lacking as a useful theory for industrial motivation. ... He found no relationship between leader-

> ship style and motivation, nor between need satisfaction and motivation.[4]

Herzberg is a theorist who created a two factor theory of motivation, which is also based on satisfaction of needs. But that formulation has not fared any better.

> One simple conclusion is that the results of these research efforts offer precious little encouragement for anyone whose theory depends upon a clear-cut relationship between satisfaction and performance. In view of the fact that his theory does assume such a relationship, support for his theory will have to come from elsewhere, and be substantial enough to refute most of the hundred-odd studies which have demonstrated faint or no relationships between job satisfaction and job performance.[5]

The weaknesses of the need concept are well known.

> The need concept is not well defined.
> It is based on unproven and unexamined assumptions.
> Descriptions of needs and need categories are ambiguous.
> Lists and categories of needs are incomplete.
> The origin of needs is disputed.
> The concept implies a lack of human adaptability.
> There is little empirical evidence for the currently popular need theories.[6]

There are also some theories which change the label of needs to motives, such as affiliation motives, achievement motives, and power motives, but that is only a different label and the same problems remain.

> Notions of energy flow did not become central to psychological theories until the late nineteenth century and, in particular, with Freud's primary insistence on an energy economy. After that, concepts of arousal, drives, motives, and their cognates became indispensable in the explanation of action. However, recent years have seen a questioning of this necessity and, at least as an attempt, it seems worthwhile to proceed with an energyless psychology that relies a little bit more on such observables as autonomic functions and less on hydraulic fictions.[7]

Not only is the fiction of need-satisfaction or motives conceptually weak and unproven by research, it assumes that an audience can be easily manipulated.

Cognitive control. However, there are alternatives. For example, Kelly contends that "A person's processes are psychologically channeled by the way he or she anticipates events."[8] In other words, prediction of future consequences is the primary force in human motivation.

> A major feature of cognitive conceptions involves the view that human beings are not only moving actively in their environments but also surveying their milieu and indeed anticipating new situations constantly by the formation of private plans or images that are then checked and rechecked as novel information is encountered. Important presentations of this cognitive emphasis on private organization of experience, on the development of centrally generated plans and anticipations, and on the fact that motivation of behavior can be generated by cognitive tendencies for clarification, reduction of ambiguity, and assimilation of complex novelty (in comparison with earlier behaviors and psychoanalytic emphasis on reduction of particular drives such as sex, thirst, or hunger) emerged in research and theory....[9] 81

Certainly we have needs, but higher mental processes are more powerful. The famous American brain researcher Wilder Penfield wrote of his grandchild,

> In the very first month you can see him – if you will take time to observe this wonder of wonders – stubbornly turning his attention to what interests him, ignoring everything else, even the desire for food or the discomfort of a wet diaper. It is evident that, already, he has a mind capable of focusing attention and evidently capable of curiosity and interest.[10]

And a renowned Russian brain researcher also found that needs were not the determiners of all action, nor even the most important actions.

> Again Luria found that by far the most interesting motivator of human behavior was not the metabolic processes that prompt us to want food, sex, and so forth. Nor was it the impact of happenings outside ourselves that captured our attention, like seeing a car wreck or reading that the rate of inflation had gone up another four points. It was the thrust of these intentions, plans, forecasts, programs "which are formed during man's conscious life, which are social in their motivation and are effected with the close participation, initially of his external, and later of his internal, speech."[11]

In other words, personal intentions and goals formed in language are more powerful in motivating people. Even simple actions are directed by higher mental processes, not lower.

> All human behavior is strictly dependent upon the higher cortical mechanisms which we are accustomed to designate as the intellectual processes. Experimentation shows that the simplest acts of behavior are intimately connected with the most complex cortical processes....[12]

Talking about needs, wants, wishes, desires, is a narrow concept of motivation. A more realistic approach is that individuals in an audience are capable of self-direction, that they make their own decisions and they are responsible for their behavior.

> Although motivation scholars have begun to appreciate the capability of humans for self-direction and self-regulation, concepts such as needs, drives, incentives, reinforcers, and the like – concepts that dominated the field for many years – continue to influence contemporary theorizing. Moreover, public understanding of "how to motivate people" is still dominated by simplistic, mechanistic conceptions of human motivation. This can be seen, for example, in college textbooks that continue to feature outdated theories of biological and situational determinism; in business seminars based on decades-old conceptions of motivational needs and incentives; and in administrative and managerial practices and procedures that fail to respect the capacity of ordinary people for self-direction, autonomous decision-making, and personal responsibility.[13]

Decision making stages. *Individuals.* Serious decision making is a process that continues over an extended period of time. Careful research reveals that non-trivial decisions don't occur all-at-once, they develop and grow in clarity and certainty through distinct stages.

> Stage 1. Appraising The Challenge. Until a person is challenged by some disturbing information or event that calls his attention to a real loss soon to be expected, he will retain an attitude of complacency about whatever course of action (or inaction) he has been pursuing.
>
> Stage 2. Surveying Alternatives. Having accepted the challenge, he begins to search his memory for alternative courses of action and seek advice and information from other people about ways of coping with the threat.

> Stage 3. Weighing Alternatives. The decision maker now proceeds to a more thorough search and evaluation, focusing on the pros and cons of each of the surviving alternatives in an effort to select the best available course of action.
>
> Stage 4. Deliberating About Commitment. After having covertly decided by telling himself that he is going to adopt a new plan of action, the decision maker begins to deliberate about implementing it and conveying his intention to others.
>
> Stage 5. Adhering Despite Negative Feedback. Stage 5...becomes equivalent to stage 1, in the sense that each unfavorable event or communication that constitutes negative feedback is a potential challenge to the newly adopted policy.[14]

Since stage one and stage five are essentially the same, there are really four stages of change. This pattern was found in individuals who made difficult decisions and carried them out successfully for very different kinds of problems, for example: giving up smoking, losing weight on a low-calorie diet, undergoing a prescribed medical treatment, career choices, and political protest actions.

Groups. Researchers have also found stages in their analysis of group decision making. Fisher labeled the four stages: orientation (of individuals to each other and the problem), conflict (over different ideas), emergence (of a best solution), and reinforcement (of the commitment of group members to the decision).[15]

Organizations. Organizations change slowly because of the large number of individuals involved, so it is not surprising to find distinct stages in studies of organizational change. Two pioneers in that research declare:

> ...the innovation process consists of problem recognition, searching for alternative solutions, matching the innovation with the organization's problem, and implementation of the innovation.[16]

Mass publics. In the field of mass communication, research traced the rate at which large numbers of people adopted new innovations. A report that summarized over 4,000 research studies of attitude and behavioral change concluded that change consists of a pattern of four stages: awareness, interest, evaluation, and trial before new methods or products were adopted.[17] It's important to note that the stage, "trial" was a mental trying out before actions were actually taken.

DECISION MAKING RESEARCH

Individual	Group	Organization	Mass public
Appraise challenge	Orientation	Problem recognition	Awareness
Survey alternatives	Conflict	Search for solutions	Interest
Weigh alternatives	Emergence	Match to organization	Evaluation
Make commitment	Reinforcement	Implementation	Trial

It is clear that a strong relationship exists between stages of individual change, small group change, organizational change, and mass public change. The first stage of appraisal, orientation, recognition, and awareness could be summed up as a process of increasing awareness.

The second stage is a survey of alternatives, involves conflict, seeks solutions, and has increased interest. This could be generalized as a process of seeking information.

The third stage evaluates alternatives, produces a solution, matches a solution to criteria, and evaluates. This could be termed, evaluating alternatives.

The last stage explores the degree of commitment, gives reinforcement, plans implementation, and is a mental trial. This could be called planning actions.

These appear to be basic processes in behavior change. Certainly, you could skip one and still make a decision, or complete them in a different order. You could also repeat some more than once, but in general, each stage seems to be important. Thus, it is proposed that these four stages could be used to design speeches which would be effective in producing change.

Psychological continuum. The four decision stages may also be related to the psychological concepts of priorities, beliefs, attitudes, and behaviors. Each one is a system and all systems have priorities. A belief ranks statements on a scale of truthfulness

> A mental decision about the nature of reality is commonly called a "belief." "A belief is a statement that we regard as true or false about our world."[18]

Beliefs combined with emotional decisions are labeled attitudes.

> Beliefs and their emotions they engender combine to form attitudes toward an object, person or event. An attitude is an inclination to respond positively or negatively.[19]

And a behavioral decision flows from attitudes. So an intention to act would include a ranking of importance, a dimension of truth or falsity, plus a dimension of emotion for or against, plus a dimension of acting or not acting. Of course in this mental, emotional, behavioral continuum there are interactions and the causal influence can go in either direction. Ilardo points out that, "It is possible for an attitude to influence a belief, similarly, intentions may influence attitudes, and behavior can influence all three.[20]

The assumption is that if a listener is in a stage of increasing awareness, then a speech that deals with priorities would be helpful. Likewise, a listener who is seeking information should be helped by a speech that deals with beliefs. So also, a listner who is evaluating alternatives should appreciate a speech that talks about attitudes, and lastly, a listener who is planning actions should value a message about behaviors.

Forms and functions. From the very beginning, the principles of public speaking (rhetoric) were conceived differently by different people. At one extreme, Plato saw it as a method of communicating universal truth to others. At the opposite extreme, were the Sophists, like Gorgias, who spoke primarily to impress others. Most teachers however, like Aristotle, were in the middle and they focused on communicating their personal truth.

So a continuum existed between an emphasis on function and an emphasis on form. One end had divisions of a speech based on the natural divisions of the subject. At the other end were divisions of a speech which were arbitrary without regard for the subject, and in the middle, the parts of a speech consisted of a general model which could be adapted to particular audiences.

FORM VERSUS FUNCTION CONTINUUM

Form follows function	Function modifies form	Function follows form
Inherent structure (Plato)	*General model* (Aristotle)	*Selections, Formulas* (Gorgias)

Plato is the best example of the search for natural, inherent structure.

> A man must first know the truth about every single subject on which he speaks or writes. He must be able to define each in terms of a universal class that stands by itself. When he has successively defined his subjects according to their specific classes, he must know how to continue the division until he reaches the point of indivisibility. He must make the same sort of distinction with reference to the nature of the soul. He must then discover the kind of speech that matches each type of nature. When that is accomplished, he must arrange and adorn each speech in such a way as to present complicated and unstable souls with complex speeches ... while the simple soul must be presented with simple speech. Not until a man acquires this capacity will it be possible to produce speech in a scientific way (rules of art), in so far as its nature permits such treatment, either for purpose of instruction or of persuasion.[21]

For him, the process of discovering truth was deduction, but note also that he recognized a difference between instruction and persuasion.

Another inherent structure was proposed by Theodorus who created the concept of "heads" of argument which is the natural clash of issues.

Closely related, is the docrine of "statis" which is the pause or state between two opposite motions – the main question in a debate.

For the Sophists, organization was not very important – many found it was effective to recite memorized passages. Some quoted maxims. Others created formulas that could be used for any occasion. For example, Protagoras used the formula: Wish, Question, Answer, Command. Another example is Appolodorus who taught that all discourse should consist of: Exordium, Narration, Argumentation, and Peroration. He would permit no other divisions or allow any less than these four.

The middle ground is best represented by Aristotle who gave a general model and then discussed how it could be modified according to different audiences. He considered all speaking persuasive in nature and described three speaking situations: law making (deliberative), courts (forensic), and ceremonial (epideictic). His model had four divisions, but could be modified for different occasions.

Exordium (deliberative, sometimes)
Statement (deliberative, rare)
Proof

Epilogue (deliberative, rare; epideictic, rare; forensic, sometimes)

So the number of divisions of a speech range from none to many, but most writers had four to seven.

Beginning, Middle, End (Plato)

Proem, Narration, Argument, Peroration (Corax)

Preamble, Narrative, Proofs, Probabilities, Confirmation, Refutation, Recapitulation (Theodorus)

Proem, Introduction, Narrative, Arguments and proofs, Epilogue (Antiphon)

Exordium, Statement, Proof, Epilogue (Lysias)

Proem, Narrative, Proof, Epilogue (Isocrates)

Proem, Prothesis, Narrative, Proof, Epilogue (Hermocrates)

The concept of no divisions was preserved as late as 1685 by Francois Fenelon,

> For the most part, divisions give only a seeming order; while they really mangle and clog a discourse, by separating it into two or three parts; which must interrupt the orator's action and the effect which it ought to produce.[22]

He did discuss different functions throughout his sermons, but stressed the unity of a speech.

> The whole discourse is one; and may be reduced to one single proposition, set in the strongest light, by various views and explications of it. This unity of design shews the whole performance at one view....[23]

The opposite extreme is a rigid formula with many divisions. This reached its climax in the Oxford University sermons in the fourteenth century with fifteen divisions.

> Finding of the theme, Allurement of the auditory, Prayer, Introduction of the theme, Division of the theme, Declaration of the parts, Confirmation of the parts, Development, Digression, Correspondance, Congruence of correspondance, Circulation, Convolution, Unification, Conclusion.[24]

Later writers gave speakers a choice in their approach to organization. Pierre Fabri gave two: one is similar to positions of argument, and the other, called distribution allowed the speaker to number the points to be presented.

Pierre de la Ramee listed three: proposition (something related to something else), syllogism, and method (order of conspicuousness).

Thomas Blunderville gave three: composite (smallest to greatest), resolution (cause and effect), and method (general to specific).

Rene Descartes also advocated the "method." He describes it as,

> The first was never to accept anything for true which I did not clearly know to be such.... The second, to divide each of the difficulties under examination into as many parts as possible, and as might be necessary for its adequate solution. The third, to conduct my thoughts in such order that, by commencing with objects the simplest and easiest to know, I might ascend by little and little, and, as it were, step by step, to the knowledge of the more complex.... And the last, in every case to make enumerations so complete, and reviews so general, that I might be assured that nothing was omitted.[25]

That logical method is contrasted with John Claude who introduced the idea of a topical order and said that sermons should have three parts. Modern writers have continued the tradition of listing several organizational patterns ranging from the logical to the topical.

In our own time we still have differences between those who advocate a flexible model and those who promote a formula. For example, John Dewey described a pattern of problem solving called reflective thinking.[26] His pattern is: suggestions, intellectualization, hypothesis, reasoning, action. But, Dewey explicitely said that the pattern should not be rigidly followed.

> The five phases, terminals, or functions of thought, that we have noted do not follow one another in a set order. ...we point out that the five phases of reflection that have been described represent only in outline the indispensable traits of reflective thinking. In practice, two of them may telescope, some of them may be passed over hurridly and the burden of reaching a conclusion may fall mainly on a single phase, which will then require a seemingly disproportionate development. No set rules can be laid down on such matters. ... In complicated cases some of the five phases are so extensive that they include definite subphases within themselves. In this case it is arbitrary whether the minor functions are regarded as parts or are listed as distinct phases.[27]

But the tendency to create simplistic formulas has always been powerful. Here are some modern examples:

Who, What, Where, When, How, Why
Advance, Build, Cite, Drive
Engage, Enlighten, Encompass, Enthuse, Enlist
Wake up, This concerns you, Generally speaking, For example, What to do
Attention, Interest, Stand, Facts, Action
Attention, Discussion, Clarification, Conclusion, Action
Exemplify, Amplify, Specify, Electrify
Hi, Trust me, You need, Hurry, Buy

A primary disadvantage of formulas is that it leads speakers to believe that not much audience analysis is necessary. They think that if you just cover all the steps, the audience will automatically be motivated. Formula speakers have a superficial concept of the speaker-audience relationship and the dynamics of a communication situation.

89

Combining the reflective thinking model with the need-satisfaction model gives the famous motivated sequence of Monroe: Attention, Need, Satisfaction, Visualization, Action.

But the reflective thinking model was not based on empirical research and need-satisfaction is a flawed concept. Therefore, from early times to modern times we see the same issues:

Inherent pattern versus arbitrary pattern,
Rigid pattern versus flexible pattern,
Simple pattern versus complex pattern,
Single pattern versus several patterns.

Organization patterns reflect differences which range from philosophical views to practical techniques. Some texts merely present a list of options.

> Not only do modern writers set no definite section of their text-books aside for the treatment of disposition (organization), but they have no clearly articulated theory of the subject.[28]

Yet, organization is extremely important to public speaking.

> ...the kinds of arrangement, when classified and made a separate study, would be to the art of communication what the forms of reasoning are to the art of judgment.[29]

This social science approach proposes that effective organization is a *progressive process* of: 1) stages of decision making, 2) information processing patterns, 3) thinking styles preference, and 4) situational demands. Each stage derives from inherent patterns based on research. Each stage also allows for creative choices in an ethical and professional way.

This process will be described in more detail in chapter 15.

Part III, Chapter 13

Preparation and Delivery Styles

Myth of preparation uniformity. This myth is that there is one best way to prepare and deliver a speech. That is contrary to research on the brain which has revealed what has been called left/right hemisphere functions in how people process information. Sperry won a Nobel Prize for his discovery.

> ...specific tests indicate functional disengagement of the right and left hemispheres with respect to nearly all cognitive and other psychic activities. Learning and memory are found to proceed quite independently in each separated hemisphere. Each hemisphere seems to have its own conscious sphere for sensation, perception, ideation, and other mental activities and the whole inner realm of gnostic experience of the one is cut off from the corresponding experiences of the other hemisphere.[1]

Information about the world is perceived by the brain in a serial order which permits us to conceive of "time" relationships and also in a parallel pattern which enables us to perceive "space" relationships.

> ...each hemisphere is specialized for a different cognitive style; the left for an analytical, logical mode for which words are an excellent tool, and the right for a holistic gestalt mode, which happens to be particularly suitable for spatial relations....[2]

Tests of intelligence and tests of personality reveal opposite variables because the two hemisphere functions complement each other. And because of those differences, messages will be understood, remembered, and influence behavior differently.

> The observable consequences of the hemispheric disconnection of the human brain show that we actually possess two brains which can function independently of each other. As a result of this duality, they may not only not react in an identical fashion to environmental stimuli, but each of them will respond only to those external influences which fall into the domain of its competence. From this it follows that any attempt to influence either the one or the other brain must be made in that hemisphere's specific "language" in order for the signal or communication to be received and processed.[3]

One hemisphere function, which for men is usually on the left side, is a cause-effect, deductive thinking pattern, and the other hemisphere function, which is more often on the right side for men, is a holistic, inductive thinking pattern. However, either of the two functions may be physically located on either side of the head, and for women the functions are equally on both sides.

Since the labels referring to physical location are gender-biased, function labels are more useful. So instead of referring to them as left or right they will be called sequencing and correlating. Many people use both functions about equally, even though others rely more on one type than the other.

Novice mistakes. There are some ways of preparing a speech which are ineffective, regardless of thinking style. For example, many beginning speakers make decisions something like this:

My success depends mostly on my subject choice.

Therefore, I need a super subject or the audience won't be interested in it.

If I can just find a great article that has really good information...

I've seen some articles like that in some popular magazines, I'll look there.

Yes, here's one that really looks great.

I'll just copy down these ideas,
...and the organization is good,

...and these examples and statistics are good too,

...and I like the beginning and ending of the article so I'll keep them also,

...many of these sentences sound good so I'll use them.

Now, I'll put it all on note cards.

I must have read over this speech a dozen times and I still can't seem to remember it.

I guess I just can't memorize.

I suppose I'll have to read this speech so I don't forget something.

If you were sitting in the audience when this speech was delivered you'd notice that if the student had succeeded in memorizing the speech, it would sound memorized; but if he reads it, it would sound read. Either way it doesn't sound very good.

You'd also notice that since the speaker is so involved in trying to remember the material, his delivery suffers. He is not aware of the verbal or visual dynamics of his presentation and doesn't look at people in the audience.

As he stands there, in actuality, *he does not have an authentic speech.* At best, the speaker is giving a poor oral interpretation of an article; at worst, he is plagerizing. In addition, he probably feels that giving a speech is a very unpleasant experience and is thinking, “I don't want to do this again.”

Shortcuts which aren't. What went wrong? His first mistake was putting too much importance on the subject choice.

Searching for the perfect subject can take too long and then he may have to grab something at the last moment as time runs out. Usually, more time should be spent on developing the subject than on choosing it. Almost any subject can be made interesting if developed well.

The second error was picking an article from a popular magazine. That's usually a mistake because they tend to be less accurate than other sources. The magazine writer is usually a reporter rather than an expert in the subject and distorts the information to make it sound more sensational than it really is. It's also possible that the article has been read by people in the audience.

But there's a more serious problem. With just one source the speaker is limited to the ideas, organization, and language, of that one article. If he were working from more than one source he could choose between the different ideas, different organization patterns, and different vocabularies. In fact, those differences would stimulate ideas of his own which would be in his own words. He would then have a speech which was the result of choices. The speech would then consist of *his* ideas, *his* organization, and *his* language.

Only some supporting material (statistic, quote, etc.) would need to be copied word-for-word. At that point, the memory burden would largely disappear because he could more easily remember his own ideas, organization, and words. The facts or examples could be read from cards.

Oral communication has a different logical and linguistic organization than an article, and it is much easier to remember than the structure and language of writing. The time it takes to get more than one source of information has a big payoff because it makes the memory task easier.

Then, when speaking, the speaker has the freedom to monitor his delivery, look at his audience, and adapt to the situation. Better preparation of content makes possible better delivery.

Thorough speech preparation makes it possible for a speaker to do his best, to feel in control, and experience the pleasure of really communicating with an audience.

The mistakes were made because the speaker had a poor concept of his relationship with his audience. He did not accept responsibility for his own ideas, or for good research. He also didn't know that each decision in speech preparation affects all the other decisions.

His fear of speaking led him to imagine exaggerated expectations on the part of the audience. He wanted material to hide behind, something he could recite. He didn't know that spending more time gathering information at the beginning would make it easier for him later to organize, remember, and present the speech. He was trying to take shortcuts rather than develop new skills. He didn't really try to achieve an authentic communication relationship.

Thinking styles. In addition to mistakes made because of inexperience, other mistakes are made because of not understanding thinking styles. Experienced speakers develop personal strategies which make their preparation efficient.

Delivery techniques aren't simply tacked on to a message. An effective speech flows naturally from an internal synthesis of your experience and personality. A dean at the University of Michigan expressed it well when he tried to describe his "best" or most effective teachers.

> What most impressed me...was how few similarities there had been among those superior mentors. ... Some were flamboyant and exuberant, but many were not. Some had a charis-

> matic platform presence, but not all. They ranged from one of the most extroverted and dynamic men I've encountered to one of the most quiet, reflective, and incisive intellects I've ever met. And in between, or perhaps in yet other dimensions, were those of wit, of gentility and grace, as well as those who were tough, cynical, or even coarse. But because, in each instance, the person had something of importance to communicate, and was concerned, conscientious, and articulate enough to say it effectively, I feel I learned appreciably from each. Beyond this, I was unable to educe any single personological attribute, let alone any composite stereotype, that would do even partial justice in describing this set of outstanding teachers.[4]

This observation is true not only of teachers, but outstanding leaders and speakers as well. Personal power comes from a personal adaptation to the challenge of speaking, and different speakers have a different synthesis of skills. Two consultants to business organizations describe their approach to leadership as follows: 95

> In Authentic Management we do not believe there is "one best way" to be or to do anything – this applies to organizations, managers, consultants, and human beings in general. What may be best for one person or system at one point in time may be wrong for the same person or system at another time. In Authentic Management, each person is encouraged to become more clearly aware of what he or she wants from others and from himself or herself, and how to go about getting it.[5]

However, a personal style develops slowly. A mature speaking style emerges out of many speaking experiences as you find an efficient mode of preparation and expression that suits you well and communicates with your audience. A style begins with the mastery of many individual speech skills, but matures with their successful integration.

> ...the law of Individual Differences reinforces the fact that no two human beings are alike, nor will they behave or react to a given stimulus, medication, diet, or stress in exactly the same, predictable manner. In spite of this knowledge, Man continues to rely heavily upon the Gaussean or bell-shaped curve when predicting, prescribing, and/or treating individuals. In so doing, Man perpetuates the unscientific practice of forever pushing, shaping, and confining individuals into the "average bell-shaped human beings" and therefore reinforces their "averaged concepts" about themselves.[6]

Development of excellence does not lead to uniformity, it increases the difference between people.

> ...when one is in the helping professions...it is of paramount importance to know, understand, and utilize nature's laws. Use of, or attempting to rely upon, the "Gaussian curve philosophy" and/or the law of averages, or trying to mold and treat individuals in relation to prescribed "recipes," constitutes a deception, not only upon the individual being treated but also upon the profession doing the treating.[7]

The profession of teaching people to communicate must recognize the positive value of individual differences and eliminate rigid models about how people should do things. An efficiency expert writes,

> The only right way is the way that's natural and right for you. Working "against the grain" is a sure road to inefficiency.... In contrast, true productivity is realized by identifying your work style and matching it to the task at hand.[8]

Monitor your personal style in preparing and delivering speeches and begin to observe the personal styles of other speakers. Awareness of a personal style of thinking is a tool leading to excellence.

Thinking styles have been given many different labels. The sequential function has also been labeled systematic and the correlating function has been called intuitive.

> McKenney and Keen investigated the way nearly 200 graduate business students solved problems. They concluded that (the) systematic style and (the) intuitive style each has unique advantages and that neither can be called superior to the other.[9]

Even though the two problem solving styles have different strengths, they are equally effective. They also show up in learning styles and teaching styles. For example, in a study of law students, law professors, and law schools, the sequential pattern was called "monopath" and the correlating pattern was labeled "polypath."

> The monopaths are apt to see a greater difference between themselves and others, while polypaths see less of a difference. The monopaths tend less to blend in, and they see their own approach as valid and true. The polypaths are much more adaptive and tolerant of high variety. Although the monopaths see a greater distance between themselves and others, this does not correlate with anxiety. They accept the difference.[10]

> ...monopaths seem to be as successful as polypaths in law school. They may have more motivation, mono-minded drive, and "follow-through." They may be more emotionally stable. They see their arguments to be valid and appropriate and therefore may press them with more vigor and skill. Polypaths are more tentative, do not reify legal abstractions so well. ... A polypathic lawyer sees human dilemmas as multidimensional and is therefore more likely to solve the problem. ...cognitive style measures differences in information processing and not whether one form of processing is better than another.[11]

Since those brain functions are so basic they apply to every stage of preparing and delivering speeches.

Personal effectiveness decisions. For several years I have administered questionnaires to public speaking students inquiring about their thinking processes as they made decisions in preparing and delivering speeches. It was obvious to me that the different strategies students used were not random, but clustered into essentially opposite patterns, and those patterns were most clearly explained by brain hemisphere research.

At the conclusion of a semester, I'd administer a questionnaire to about a hundred students. Then I would analyze the results, revise the questionnaire, and give the new version to new students at the end of the following semester. So gradually, over time the important differences were more clearly identified. The last sample I took consisted of 353 students. The results are reported in percentages at the beginning of each chapter in part II.

I also wanted to know how my thinking style test compared to the Myers-Briggs personality test. A sample of 219 showed:

PERSONALITY AND THINKING STYLES

Myers-Briggs	Sequencers	Correlators	Bilaterals
Extrovert/Introvert	**51**/28	**41**/16	**63**/20
Thinking/Feeling	30/**49**	19/**38**	38/**45**
Sensing/Intuition	**62**/17	18/**39**	39/**44**
Judgment/Perception	**57**/22	17/**40**	32/**51**

1) About twice as many speakers were extroverts as introverts.
2) About twice as many were feelers rather than thinkers.
3) Sequencers were more sensors and judgers

4) Correlators were more intuitors and perceivers.
5) Bilaterals tend to be more equally divided.

So, this is what speakers tend to have in common:

Extroverts are friendly, talkative, easy to know. They express emotions easily and need relationships. They feel pulled outward by external conditions and are energized by other people.

Feelers take an immediate and personal view and go by personal convictions. They are concerned with harmony and are good at understanding people.

And this is where speakers tend to differ from each other – their personal preparation and speaking style:

Sensors look at parts and pieces, *intuitors* look at patterns and relationships. Sensors prefer handling practical matters, intuitors prefer imagining possibilities. Sensors like things that are measurable, intuitors like being inventive. Sensors like set procedures and routines, intuitors like change and variety.

Judgers like order and structure and *perceivers* like going with the flow. Judgers like to have things under control, but perceivers like to experience life as it happens. Judgers like being decisive, perceivers like surprises. Judgers like clear limits, perceivers like freedom to explore.

As a speaker, you should be familiar with the opposite patterns. You need to discover what is realistic and effective for you and what is not. You may be able to use either style equally well, and that is useful to know also.

Part III, Chapter 14

Getting Subjects

Personal effectiveness decisions. There are roughly equal numbers of people who are very analytical thinkers and those who are very holistic thinkers.

Some follow a deductive approach, some are more inductive

A few begin with an objective analysis of the audience, but twice as many find a subjective relating to the audience more powerful. Many speakers choose a subject by their own interests and then adapt it to the audience.

It has been assumed that everyone has a difficult time thinking of subjects. Actually, for a third of the population the problem is the opposite – they think of too many subjects and their problem is choosing the best one.

About half the population find it easier to begin with choosing a subject, about half find it easier to begin with choosing a purpose – obviously, it can be done either way.

The relative amount of time spent (and also the relative difficulty) choosing a subject compared with organizing it is different for different people.

Myth of demographic analysis. This myth is that group membership variables help you select a speech subject. The most detailed list of audience factors is found in *The Psychology of Speaker's Audiences.*[1] (*See next page*).

DEMOGRAPHIC FACTORS

Environmental factors	Group-membership factors	
Physical surroundings	Age	Geographic
Predispositions	Sex	Political
Self-selection	Race	Social
Sense of fitness	Education	Religion
Conformity influence	Occupation	Culture
Polarization	Socioeconomic	Avocation

PSYCHOLOGICAL FACTORS

Speaker-image factors	Listener-motivational factors
Perceived friendship	Expressive needs
Perceived authority	Commitments
Perceived trustworthiness	Values
Motivational expectancies	Personality
Ability expectancies	Language expectancies

Comparing each of these factors the author concludes the demographic factors have limited usefulness.

> The most salient audience factors determining outcomes of speech communication vary from situation to situation. These are only seldom the factors cited in speech textbooks – such as age, sex, education, religion, and various affiliations.[2]

> In reviewing the many factors which influence listener contribution to communication outcomes, it should be remembered that not all are important in each speaker-listener transaction and that *speaker-image* and *listener-motivational* factors will be crucial more frequently than *environmental* and *group-membership* factors.[3]

Today, in our pluralistic society, values and attitudes cut across demographic and social groups. You no longer can confidently predict what a person may believe because of environmental factors or group membership factors.

Groups typically have only a few characteristics that bind them together. Even when a group coalesces around a single cause, any group of people has more differences among them than similarities.

However, these factors do alert you to language choices. You certainly don't want to insult or offend any group of individuals. So knowledge of social groupings helps you adapt your message to the audience, but first you have to come up with your message.

Audience image. Try to learn as much as possible about the audience when you receive a request to speak. The time limit, facilities, and purpose are all important.

> Everything the effective speaker does by way of preparation for speaking – during any and all of the steps that textbooks normally recommend – is done in response to his image of the audience.[4]

If possible, find out what they think about you – their expectations, their questions. Create a mental picture of who they are and what they think.

> Certain emotions, attitudes, and judgments begin to form in the speaker's mind at this instant of recognition of an audience-to-be. These feelings and decisions, influenced by the image of the prospective audience, in turn affects the total process of the speaker's preparation and speaking.[5]

Four speech components. Many people say the hardest part of preparing a speech is "getting a subject" or "getting started." The reason it is difficult is that getting a subject is not one single problem, but instead it is four separate tasks. What you have to do is: l) select ideas, 2) select imagery, 3) select a speech nucleus, and 4) select a subject label.

Select ideas and imagery. It is extremely helpful to think of all the statements in your speech as being of two kinds, ideas or imagery. Ideas usually express relationships or how something is related to something else: it's more important, it came first, I like it, etc.

Imagery consists of things like: examples, facts, quotes, statistics, and stories. An important principle to remember when you are gathering material for a speech is that generally, you should have at least one item of specific imagery for every general idea.

Select a subject label and a nucleus. One decision sets the limits to the information. You can only talk about so much in the time you have, so how broad do you want the subject to be? That decision is called the speech subject. It is the label you put on the subject matter to narrow down the number of ideas you will talk about.

The other decision picks out the most important single idea. It is the sharp focus of your message and is often called the thesis, though the term speech nucleus is more suggestive. Think of a speech being like an atom with an idea statement for a nucleus and all the other ideas and imagery in the speech being held in place by that nuclear thought. The nucleus is the most important thing you want the audience to remember. While the subject label decision determines the breadth of your speech, the speech nucleus decision determines the depth of your message.

Either one could come first. Suppose you have already gathered some material on a general subject. You then would search among the ideas to find which statement best expresses what is most important, that's your nucleus. On the other hand, maybe you already have a key thought you wish to relate (nucleus). Now you must decide how much other material should be added until you have enough to round out the subject.

When asked to speak, some people say their mind goes blank. That really doesn't happen because possibilities occur to you, the problem is that you're really not sure if they're good enough. You may think of an idea, but don't know if you can build a speech out of it. You may know a great story (imagery) you'd like to tell, but aren't certain what kind of point you would make with it. You may even have a particular point of view (speech nucleus) you'd like to give, but don't know how to support it. Or you may think of a good subject label, but don't know enough about it. The real problem is that any one component is not enough. All four factors go together to form the genesis of a speech.

The biggest mistake you can make in this beginning stage is that when you think of one of the four components you discard it because you don't have the other three. Don't discount an immediate impression; try to think of other material to go with it. An entire speech does not flash full-blown into your mind. It comes a piece at a time, so don't throw away any pieces.

Title. Related to the subject label is the title, which could be any type of statement. It is a way of advertising the speech beforehand and also a way of helping the audience remember the speech afterward. You could use the subject label, the speech nucleus or any statement that arouses interest.

Speaker-audience relationship. It's not a question of which comes first, audience-analysis or self-analysis, speeches come from the dynamic interaction of both. There is a tension created between these two mental images. Ask yourself, what are the possible questions or problems people in the audience might be having and what is some possible information or advice you might be able to give them. The creative tension between speaker-image and audience-image produces speech subjects.

> The juxtaposition of vision (what we want) and a clear picture of current reality (where we are relative to what we want) generates what we call "creative tension:"a force to bring them together, caused by the natural tendency of tension to seek resolution. The essence of personal mastery is learning how to generate and sustain creative tension in our lives.[6]

Imagine a typical member of the audience. Visualize that person clearly. Mentally, ask him or her provocative questions: What do you think about most of the time? How do you spend your money? How do you waste your time? What would you want your children to do better than you have done? What really frightens you? How could I help you? Your speech preparation is a mental dialogue you carry on with that imaginary listener who you will meet at a predetermined time.

> For the speaker trying to understand his audience, the question is ... "What are my interests in the lives of the listeners and to what extent do they know it?" The answer is not easy. However genuine interest usually communicates itself readily and almost always earns response in kind. Interest begets interest.[7]

The same is true of the beliefs you share, the common attitudes you hold, and similar things you plan to do. That is the way you can relate to the audience and they can relate to you at a more personal level. The famous psychologist, Carl Rogers, said:

> What is most personal is most general. There have been times when in talking with students or staff, or in my writing, I have expressed myself in ways so personal that I have felt I was expressing an attitude which it was probable no one else could understand, because it was so uniquely my own.... In these instances I have almost invariably found that the very feeling which has seemed to me most private, most personal and hence

> most incomprehensible by others, has turned out to be an expression for which there is a resonance in many other people. It has led me to believe that what is most personal and unique in each of us is probably the very element which would, if it were shared or expressed, speak most deeply to others.[8]

Originality. The speaker's task is not finding a subject – they are not laying around. You create speech subjects. Your task is to figure out what aspects of a particular subject can be made interesting to the audience.

While people are different and have different viewpoints, cultural differences tend to be less powerful than our common humanity.

Two audience types. Is this a new audience or is it an audience with whom you're familiar? The new audience/same message model is the one encountered most by salespeople, entertainers, politicians, evangelists, and motivational speakers.

The same audience/new message model of preparation is different. It includes ministers, managers, and leaders in organizations. But sometimes you do both, like a teacher who faces the same class for a semester or year and then meets a new class the following semester or year.

To prepare a message for a new audience you can use ideas, evidence, and illustrations from a previous speech, but some changes will need to be made. The language will need to be modified to relate better to a different group. The organization may need to be modified to fit different time limits. And your delivery will probably have to change to fit a different location and number of people.

Giving a new message to a familiar audience presents a different challenge. You know their interests and they know your interests, you have received feedback on your ideas from previous speeches and therefore you can take advantage of the common ground that has been established. They are familiar with your speaking style which includes your use of language and your delivery. But, you'll certainly need new ideas, and new evidence or illustrations.

With the new audience model much of what you say is repeated from other presentations, but you still try out different ideas and imagery and eliminate what doesn't work. There is a continual process of improvement: 1) You have a repertory of tested material that you know is effective, and 2) you develop some new material to try out on each new audience.

Whenever you know beforehand that you will be giving several speeches to the *same* audience you realize it requires that you search continually for new speech material. Professionals usually have an ongoing program of reading and/or interacting with different people to give them new ideas. Often they develop a long-range strategy: several speeches could develop a theme, or cover subdivisions of a subject, or analyze a sequence of principles, etc.

Therefore, in a speech class you definitely should *select all your speech subjects at the beginning*. Picking one subject, speaking on it, and then picking the next subject and speaking on it, is a very inefficient way of working. While you are preparing your first speech you might run onto some information that could be used in one of the future speeches you have tentatively chosen. You might hear something on the news, or in a lecture, you may see an article, or have a conversation with someone which suggests ideas that could be used. So while you are concentrating on one speech the others can simmer on the back burner.

Most of the time speakers are asked to speak on their expertise. The audience expects you to talk about what you have done or what you know best. Sometimes they even want you to repeat what you have told some other audience. What does that tell you? You were asked because of your credibility (expertise and trust). You'll continue to be asked in the future if you keep that reputation for credibility.

There are generally two ways to satisfy an audience's desire to hear something original. Either give them something new that they didn't know, or give them a new way to look at what they do know: new information or a new perspective. Both are appreciated by an audience.

Probes for brainstorming. While one set of probes is suggestive, it's very powerful to arbitrarily match two sets of probes.

Suppose one probe was *news* and the other was *theory-practice.* What occurs to you? I thought of how much information in a newspaper is not "news" – advertisements, want ads, and comics. I also thought about what percentage of readers write letters to an editor. You probably were thinking of other things – good!

Perhaps I had already decided to give a speech on UFO's. If I selected the probe *new-old* I would think of a sighting reported by Alexander Hamilton. I also thought of the Air Force investigation, and if the probe were *cause-effect* I would think of the changes in the general public's attitude toward space travel.

Remember that any subject could be matched with any probe to generate a subject label, speech nucleus, idea, or imagery for a speech. For example, take the general subject "work" and match it with different speech purposes.

For awareness, you might think of how workers get a tax cut just before an election and an increase in taxes after the election is over.

With information, you might think of the statistical procedure for measuring unemployment or the measure of productivity called the G.N.P. or the G.D.P.

For argument, you might remember that some groups are trying to limit work to a four day week, yet other individuals are trying to find second jobs (moonlighting).

And action could make you think of how some work produces stress and ruins health, yet to reduce stress you can use exercise which is called a "workout.'

Whether this technique helps you depends on how conscientiously you use the probes. Simply reading through a list will not help you at all. Creativity is related to the time, the place, and your mental attitude.

Select a time. You are creative when you are not rushed, don't have an appointment, or worries on your mind. Just prior to going to sleep or just upon awakening are particularly productive times for many people.

Select a place. The best places are where you are alone and will not be distracted. Perhaps when you are resting or when engaged in a routine activity like mowing a lawn or listening to music.

Free associate. You could assume a passive mental state where you let any thought or feeling arise in your consciousness. You could imagine scenes or pictures. In the back of your mind you have a monitor asking, "Could I use that in my speech?"

Don't rush. Creativity doesn't happen on demand. You create the conditions that make it possible and remain alert for its signs. Preparing a speech is not just an intellectual process, it also involves your feelings. Capitalize on emotional relationships to unlock creativity and memory.

Resource search. A great source of material for speeches is the library, but many people have an aversion to using it because it takes them too long to find what they want. So to develop a time-saving strategy, let's look at how information comes into a library.

Some expert discovers something. She will probably tell her colleagues and other people with the same interests. That may be at a conference of such individuals. It could appear in a professional newsletter.

Then it will get published in a professional journal that is circulated to a wider readership in that professional field.

Then it will be printed in a magazine which caters to the well-educated reader with wide interests. These are half-way versions between the very technical writing and the easy-to-read magazines. Later it shows up in mass circulation magazines.

Even if that process occurs very quickly – some articles in professional journals are summarized in newspapers and TV broadcasts – the important thing is that different journals will vary greatly in detail and accuracy.

Your goal is to discover the *most accurate* and *most recent* information in the library. That is the priority for speeches.

Thus, the most efficient search strategy for speeches is to begin with the professional journals. Go to the current periodical section of your library. Look for the professional journals dealing with the subject you have chosen for your speech. Or, if you haven't picked a subject, that's a good place to browse. The popular magazines should generally be avoided, because they are not very accurate. One insider at the White House writes,

> As for newspaper or (popular) magazine accounts, they are sometimes worse than useless when they purport to give the inside history of decisions; their relation to reality is often considerably less than the shadows in Plato's cave. I have too often seen the most conscientious reporters attribute to government officials views the exact opposite of which the officials are advocating within the government to make it possible for me to take the testimony of journalists in such matters seriously again.[9]

> There is, ...especially for *Time,* a kind of gag rule which seriously inhibits free reporting. On a typical newspaper, aside from writing editorials, an editor usually confines himself to polishing and refining copy coming from the field; the story published is basically a product of the man at the scene of the story. With *Time,* the reverse is true. Copy filed from reporters in the field is primarily stimulus to editorial imagination. Testimony on this point from defectors from the magazine is unanimous.[10]

Once you locate a quality journal that covers your subject, you'll have the best information in the library on that subject – the most accurate and the most recent. Following are some examples of the kind of quality journals you'll discover.

Symposium type journals. These scholarly journals dedicate each issue to one subject. All the articles by the different authors discuss the same problem. A source that does the same thing for newspaper editorials is, *Editorial Research Reports.* You'll find that there will be more than enough material for a speech, or even several speeches. Below are a few examples.

The American Behavioral Scientist
The Annals of the American Academy of Political and Social Science
Law and Contemporary Problems
Philosophical Forum
Prospects
Sociological Symposium
World Health
Indiana Social Studies Quarterly
Journal of Social Issues
The Center Magazine
Congressional Digest
Current History
Daedalus
Impact of Science on Society

General commentary journals. These comment on what's happening in the world, but they do it better than the popular news-magazines. Some give a conservative point of view and some have a liberal point of view. Others may be moderate or radical, but you'll find stimulating ideas between their covers. Pick both a conservative and a liberal journal to compare their ideas on the same subject.

Atlas
Challenge
Commentary
Conservative Digest
Contemporary Crises
The New Republic
Dissent
The Nation
National Review
The New World Review
The Progressive
Schism
Skeptic
World Press Review

Discipline or subject matter journals. These magazines cover many subjects in their respective fields and are very accurate. This is just a sampling to show the range that exists and to arouse your curiosity.

The American Atheist
The Bulletin of the Atomic Scientists
Human Behavior
Index on Censorship

Christianity Today
The Coevolution Quarterly
Consumer
Contemporary Education
Correction Today
The Department of State Bulletin
Psychology Today
Public Welfare
Scientific American
Sciquest
Social Policy
Social Work Today
The Futurist
Journal of Individual Psychology
The Journal of Parapsychology
Nutrition Today
Personnel and Guidance Journal
Politics Today
Problems of Communism
History Today
Environment
Etc.
Family Health
Farm Journal
First World
Gifted Child Quarterly

Computer searches follow the same principles. When using a computer it is even more critical to use the strategy of "most accurate, most recent." Typing in a request for a general subject will result in hundreds of references. That's not very helpful. Your request needs to be strategic: 1) there are fewer journals than books, 2) many journals exist in each field, so look for sub-divisions, and 3) find out which journals are the most respected.

You may see a relationship between brainstorming with language probes and computer searches with key words. Research always involves creativity. The internet has some valuable information, but it also has false information. The advantage of printed material is that it has an established reputation for accuracy. The publisher and editor and writer's reputation are on the line. With the internet, you can't be sure if the source is who it claims to be. Be cautious, there's a lot of garbage on the internet.

Interviews can be more helpful than books or periodicals. In fact, the occasion of giving a speech is a good excuse to interview people who you would like to talk to, but have never before had a specific reason. You now have that reason. It is easier to obtain an interview when you have a specific purpose.

You should determine exactly what you would like to know before you contact a minister, businessperson, school official, scientist, political figure, etc. Plan your questions carefully so you do not impose on their time, and indicate you are gathering information for a speech when you call for an appointment.

Remember, if you are reluctant about speaking with public personalities, that they often have information that can be found nowhere else. Many things they could tell you are not written down in books or magazines. In fact, they may have information that they wish were more widely known and may welcome your visit.

This does not mean that you should only consider persons in the spotlight. Many public agencies have knowledgeable individuals who do not come to the attention of the public, but who could provide very valuable information.

Surveys. You can collect opinions from a sample of people in the community or special groups who are affected by different events. A survey is a great help but you must analyze the results carefully. The questions should be carefully worded so that you can get the information you want. Seriously consider gathering opinions from people. That is probably the most overlooked source of excellent information for speeches.

Part III, Chapter 15

Organizing Plans

Personal effectiveness decisions. There are about an equal number of speakers who organize with a priority on logic as opposed to a priority on interestingness – content focused or relationship focused. Both are equally important, but people tend to have a bias for one more than the other.

The importance of a strength in external, pencil-and-paper organizing skill compared to a strength in internal, mental construct organizing skill can not be over-emphasized for public speaking. This dictates not only organization patterns, but rehearsal strategies, and the necessity for memory aids when speaking.

Originally, when the question was asked about use of an outline, about half of any group said they do not use one, unless forced to do so. When the idea-imagery outline was introduced, the numbers changed to about a third for the logical, a third for the idea-imagery, and a third who still found little or no benefit from any outline.

About a third try to improve their language expressiveness in their speeches.

More than half plan their delivery. That's encouraging, but more speakers could benefit from that practice.

Myth of the logical outline. The myth is that a deductive pattern is the best way to organize a speech. But, if you ask a class of students how many of them will write a paper first and then make the outline afterwards, you'll find almost half of the class will raise their hands.

Even those who create the outline first, often will use the system of symbols, but ignore the logical principles on which the system is based. That isn't because they don't care about doing a good job, it's because that's not the most effective way for them to manage information.

Limitations. The traditional outline is most useful for general-to-specific patterns, argument-support patterns, and first-to-last patterns. But other organizational patterns can not be used. It is not very helpful if you want to begin with a fact or illustration and follow it with a major point. It doesn't allow you to compare different ideas or arguments before discussing the reasons or evidence. And it doesn't permit you to change the natural time order of events. In short, you can't arrange your ideas for their psychological impact.

TRADITIONAL VERSUS NON-TRADITIONAL PATTERNS

Traditional patterns	Non-traditional patterns
General-to-Specific	*Specific-to-General*
Main idea	Illustration
Sub-idea	Sub-idea
Illustration	Main idea
Argument-Support	*Argument-Argument*
Pro argument	Pro argument 1
Reasons	Con argument 1
Evidence	Reasons or evidence
Con argument	Pro argument 2
Reasons	Con argument 2
Evidence	Reasons or evidence
First-to-Last	*Variable Time Order*
First event	Present description
Second event	Past description
Third event	Future description
etc.	etc.

You couldn't make a division where there is only one subpoint instead of two or more. You couldn't use a reversal or surprise switch in your development. And you couldn't use more than one organizational principle to create divisions in your speech. An alternative to the traditional outline is the idea-imagery outline.

Content plan. Just standing in front of a lot of people and talking is not a speech. A speech is a previously prepared message designed for a large number of listeners to achieve some purpose(s). It may be a written speech not yet delivered, but it was written with the intention of being presented to an audience. There may be only one person listening, but the message was prepared with the expectation that more would be present.

So the essence of a speech is its structure, it is designed to fit the physical and psychological constraints inherent in a situation with a live audience. A professional is also expected to be able to create a speech structure which is dynamic – designed so it can be rapidly modified, if necessary.

Even though you can't control what will be "heard" by the audience, you can target the decision making processes strategically to give you the best chance of accomplishing your purpose. *The different speech models are applied in a particular situation to the degree that you know the decision making questions in the minds of the listeners.*

Awareness speech. Most special occasions mark a highlight or an important change. Something significant is going to happen or has happened. Consequently, most of these speeches are about something beginning or something ending.

The speech challenges our experience, it changes our viewpoint, disturbs our apathy, or makes a comment about our goals. Its essence is to change the organizational structure of our values by suggesting different priorities to us. While the awareness speech is often given on special occasions, it's not limited to those times. It is appropriate anytime an audience needs to be provoked or alerted. The goal is for a member of the audience to say, "That's important."

Awareness speeches range from humorous to serious, from routine to unique. They note ceremonial occasions and times of crisis. Generally, they highlight the meaning of an event. You choose words to express the essence of a situation, you arrange data to create a new perception, appreciation or ideal, a different view of reality.

Common components of an awareness speech are the following:

Describe the occasion.

Explain the significance or meaning of the occasion.

Describe the person and/or group of people involved.

Recall past events or actions.

Point to future events or actions.

Sometimes, create a theme.

These characteristics are not in any particular order and not every awareness speech will have all of them.

Introduction (welcome). When you are going to introduce or welcome someone you should talk to the person beforehand and ask if there is something he or she would like included in your remarks. Get accurate information and pronounce his or her name correctly. Usually you say the name at the very end of your introduction so the applause that normally follows an introduction will be associated with the name of the person.

Since an introduction is the meeting of at least two people who don't know each other, it's appropriate to describe not only the person you are welcoming, but also the audience who is extending the welcome through you. Point out the purpose for being together. The speaker will often respond briefly to your introduction before starting his or her speech.

Presentation (commencement). Usually when an award is to be given to a recipient the presentation is brief. But a commencement speech is a formal presentation in an academic setting and considerably longer. Obviously, past achievements should be emphasized. The nature of the award (criteria) should be explained and new goals may be suggested. When you call the person forward, first shake hands and then hand them the award with your left hand.

The appropriate response is to thank those who gave the award and thank those who helped you earn it. You could mention anecdotes or unknown events that occurred in the process of your work and also what the award means to you.

Nomination (acceptance). A speech to nominate someone will identify the person at the beginning unless everyone knows who you are nominating, then you could leave the candidate's name until the end. Your task is to give reasons why that person will do a good job. And the more reasons you give the better. Later, the same kind of information could be used in the campaign.

The acceptance speech usually covers the same ground. That is, the reasons given in the nominating speech (knowledge, caring, etc.) can be demonstrated by the candidate in his or her acceptance speech.

Tribute (farewell). These speeches are the flip side of an introduction speech and sometimes a token gift is presented. Both the tribute and farewell speech may recall accomplishments and little known information about handicaps or trials that were overcome. They dwell on shared experience, good wishes and hope for a future reunion. The response may also express the same things in a reciprocal way.

When a tribute is to someone who is deceased the speech is called an eulogy. The eulogy is perhaps the best example of restructuring people's awareness. It summarizes the events of a person's life. It may suggest a theme or relationship which best epitomizes the appropriate memory of the individual.

Inaguration (dedication). Typically, you inaugurate a person or process and you dedicate a building or object. These speeches are usually a little longer than the presentation speech, but are similar. The emphasis is on insightful description, thanking people, past accomplishments and new directions or goals.

Challenge (inspiration). The challenge speech describes a problem, but does not necessarily suggest a solution. It points out how "what is" differs from "what should be." That frustrating lack of closure unleashes great energy to fill the void. The audience starts thinking of solutions even before you complete your talk.

An inspirational speech differs only slightly in approach. If a group is discouraged, over-extended or worried, the emphasis is not so much on the difficult problem, but on the fact that a solution is possible. Even if you don't offer a solution, you offer hope and express confidence in the individuals. Previous challenges successfully overcome are powerful reminders of hidden strengths. Sometimes you can both challenge and inspire in the same speech.

Announcement. Most announcements are quickly forgotten, but they need not be. Give a reason why everyone should listen to your announcement. Give the particulars (time, place, dress, cost, etc.). Give some elaboration or description. Suggest some examples of things that would be particularly enjoyable. At the end, repeat the important details before sitting down.

Entertainment. There is a great difference between a speech to entertain and a comedy routine. Because of our exposure to comedians on TV, many people feel that if they can't be as funny as them then they shouldn't try to entertain. First of all, most of those performers have writers working for them and second, they are not making a speech, a comedy routine is merely a string of jokes loosely tied together.

The characteristics of the speech are that it makes a serious point in a creative way. But this speech does not have to provoke great laughter to be successful. Entertainment is much broader than just comedy.

Information speech. The speech that informs is the speech that makes concepts clear. A listener should be able to repeat the main ideas or assertions at the conclusion of the speech. This is a speech on a non-controversial subject. You present the information in such a way that the audience has confidence in its accuracy. You introduce new ideas in a straight forward, non-argumentative manner. The audience may know it is uninformed or it may not realize that it has incorrect assumptions or beliefs about the subject. You may point out inconsistencies or wrong applications of ideas they thought they understood.

It differs from the awareness speech where you can invent a concept, context or point of view. An information speech must describe actual relationships that exist between concepts in the most simple, functional way so that everyone in the audience would say, "Yes, that's the way it really is." To really know something you must know the internal relationships between its parts and also the external relationships to other subjects. Information speeches sometimes are labeled: presentations, reports, briefings, lectures, or demonstrations.

Argument speech. This speech calls for evaluating choices or options, and that creates an argument. An argument speech is a reasoned statement. Using emotion in this speech borders on the unethical. Typically, these speeches discuss both sides of a question.

An argument requires two elements: reasoning and evidence. In simplified form, the structure of reasoning is "Something is related in a particular way to something else." X causes Y, P is similar to Q, etc. Reasoning claims a particular relationship exists, such as: cause, generalization, analogy, sign, or definition. You could visualize reasoning as links of a chain. A statement which says one concept is related to another concept in a particular way is sometimes called a proposition.

REASONING

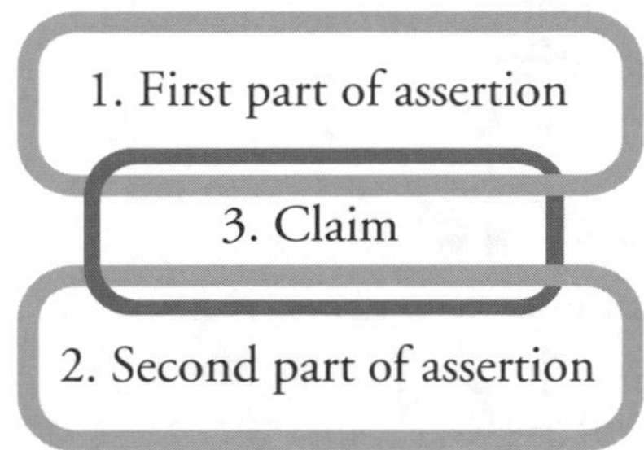

Evidence consists of very accurate information, particularly facts or statistics. To test the accuracy of the data you look closely at how the particular instance is described; who is the person making the statement and what is the source, or under what conditions was the observation made? A particular instance is only useful when it is backed up by a competent source under optimum conditions. You could visualize evidence as an arrow.

EVIDENCE

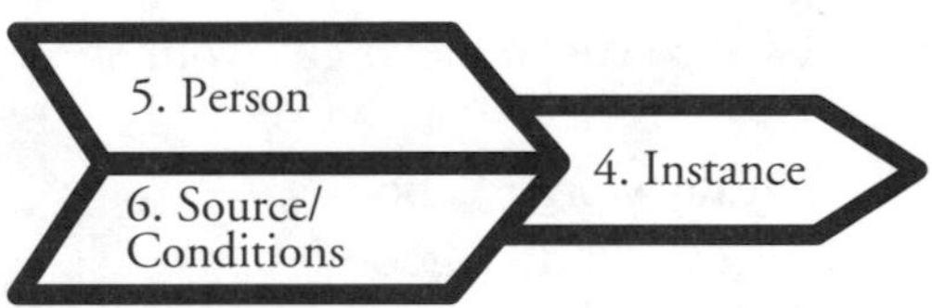

You combine reasoning with evidence to make an argument that will attract serious attention.

ARGUMENT

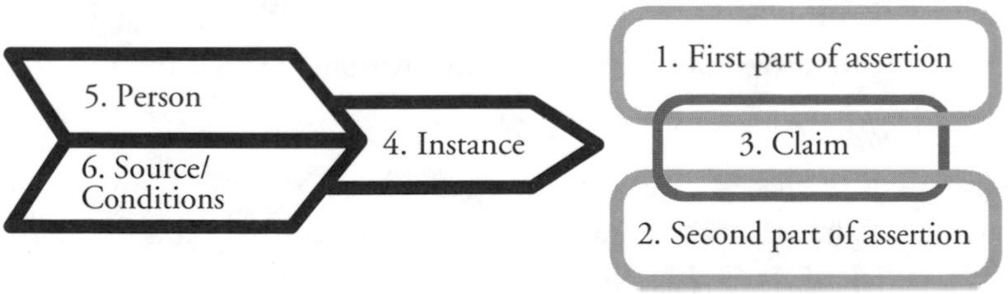

This diagram allows you to analyze an argument by examining the important parts for their precision. For the first part you would ask questions about definitions of important words. For the second part you would also ask about definitions of terms. The third element is to determine the relationship that is claimed between parts one and two. Under the fourth part you would ask about the relevance of the instances and the number of them. The fifth part inquires about the authority or credentials of the person making the assertion. And the sixth part includes questions about time, place, publication, etc. Of course there may also be counter-evidence.

ARGUMENT WITH COUNTER-EVIDENCE

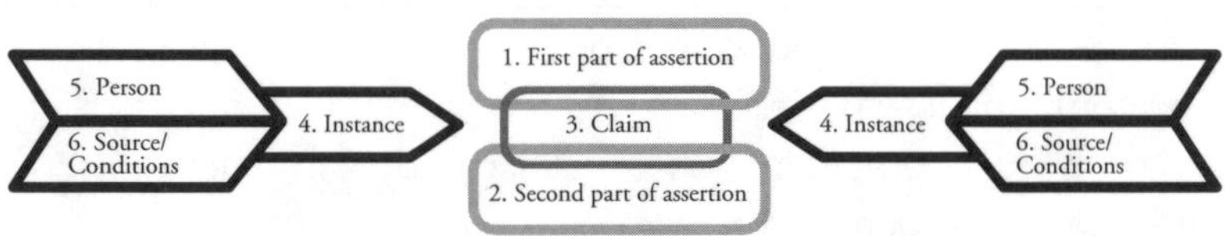

Let's consider some examples. Suppose you overheard a conversation between two students discussing their speech class:

Liann: Say, Maren, I see you're going to give your speech first on Monday.

Maren: Yeah, and I'm really worried about it!

Liann: Aw, you're smart, you'll do a good job.

Maren: I really don't feel ready to speak.

Liann: Well, you're more ready than the rest of us. You've had all kinds of speaking experiences in student body offices and being president of your sorority, so you're a good speaker.

Maren: The thing that bothers me is knowing how to say what I want to say. I don't know if I can find the right words or explain exactly what I mean.

Liann: C'mon, don't kid me. You always get A's on your English themes – you won't have any trouble with your language.

After Monday's Class ....

Maren: Boy, did I bomb on that speech!

Liann: What do you mean? Everyone applauded when you finished. Everyone liked your speech.

Maren: I don't think I did very well.

Liann: Now look! You spoke with confidence, your speech was well organized, you had strong gestures and you moved the audience – that was a good speech. Besides, you've always done well. You're just a good speaker. Some people can speak and some can't – like Jim, I can't listen to him at all.

Maren: Why not? I think he does well.

Liann: Well, I had another class with him and I saw him cheat on a test so I can't believe a word he says.

Maren: But you don't have to know if someone's honest to judge whether he speaks well; take politicians for instance, I don't know if the president is honest or not, but I like the way he speaks.

Liann: Yeah, I agree, he is a good speaker. My teacher said he gives good speeches. He must have taken a speech class to do so well. I'm glad we have a speech class.

Maren: Why do you say that?

Liann: Well, it's hard to get in. Everyone wants a speech class. But did you hear that they may eliminate public speaking as a required course?

Maren: No, why would they do that?

Liann: I don't know, but that's really a mistake if they do it because it's always been a requirement and if everyone else had to take speech then I think all the new students should take it too.

Maren: Well, that's just your opinion....

Liann: No, I have proof. 64% of successful people say that a speech class helped them.

Maren: Oh, I didn't know that.

That simple interchange of thoughts consists of many assertions being made and some reasons why those assertions should be considered valid. We'll place some of them in the diagram to demonstrate the relative strengths or weaknesses of the reasoning.

TESTING REASONING. *Cause.* "You're smart, you'll do a good job." In essence it states that if you're smart then you will be a good speaker, or being smart causes a person to be a good speaker. Our diagram shows us the questions which can be asked.

1. Do we know what "being smart" means?

2. Do we know what "being a good speaker" means?
3. The claim is that part one causes or makes the second part happen.
4. Do we have instances which show that some smart people are good speakers? Are some smart people not good speakers? Or, are some good speakers not smart people?
5. Do we know if the person making this assertion is an expert on being smart or on good speaking?
6. Do we know under what conditions this is supposed to be true? Speaking in a classroom? Speaking when sufficient time is given for preparation? etc.

On the basis of the questions raised about the proposition you can decide if the statement has any merit or not.

Generalization. "You've had all kinds of speaking experiences in student body offices and being president of your sorority, so you're a good speaker." This is a generalization made from several instances.

1. The kinds of speaking are defined by the instances given, she must mean speaking in leadership positions. What do all the instances have in common?
2. What does good speaking mean? That you're popular? That you get elected to offices?
3. This makes a general statement based on examples.
4. Are there enough instances to satisfy us? Are the instances good examples of speaking experience? Were there speeches where she did not do well?
5. Who says the speaking was good? Members of the organizations? Objective observer?
6. What conditions were present? Was she speaking to friends or strangers? Was she in leadership positions because of other abilities?

Analogy. "You always get A's on your English themes – you won't have any trouble with your language." Here is an analogy between writing and speaking. The assertion is that if you write well you will speak well.

1. Good writing is defined by A's on themes.
2. What is good language when speaking?
3. Analogy compares one thing with something else.
4. Does she always get A's?

5. Who is the English teacher? Who is the speech teacher?
6. Are theme requirements similar to speaking requirements?

Sign. "Everyone applauded when you sat down. Everyone liked your speech" Applause is a sign that the audience liked the speech, or is it? That's the question.

1. We'll assume we know what applause is.
2. We'll assume we know what "liking a speech" means.
3. Sign reasoning implies that the two always occur together.
4. How many applauded? How loud? How long? Do we know of instances when a bad speech was applauded or, a good speech that was not applauded?
5. Who claims applause means a good speech?
6. Does applause in a classroom mean the same as applause elsewhere?

Definition. "You spoke with confidence, your speech was well organized, you had strong gestures and you moved the audience – that was a good speech." Here we have an implicit definition of what a good speech is.

1. We are told the parts of the definition, but do we know what each of the words mean?
2. This is the concept being defined.
3. Definition means that most people agree the two parts of the assertion mean the same thing.
4. Are there other criteria like significant subject matter or good material?
5. Is Liann an authority?
6. Does the criteria apply only to a classroom speech? An impromptu speech? etc.

TESTING FOR FALLACIES. The arguments just listed consist of reasoning that is acceptable if the evidence supports them. But, there are some other kinds of reasoning that are rejected because the relationship between the two parts of the assertion is faulty or fallacious. Here are some common fallacies.

All or nothing. "Some people can speak and some can't." It implies that there are no other options or degrees of difference. Is it really necessary to choose between only the two alternatives given?

1. What is the definition of "speaking well?"
2. What is the definition of "not speaking well?"
3. All or nothing means that only those two categories exist.
4. Are there any average speakers? Or are there some speakers who sometimes speak well and sometimes don't?
5. Who says?
6. Under what conditions? Always?

Ad hominum. "I saw him cheat on a test so I can't believe a word he says." This argument is that because he has done one wrong thing, then other things he does are wrong also. Ad hominum means attacking the person. This is similar to saying "Consider the source," or "Where there's smoke there's fire."

1. Did it only appear to be cheating or was it really cheating?
2. What kind of honesty in speaking is implied?
3. Ad hominum looks at the character of the person in some other context than the one under discussion.
4. Are there instances of people who cheat and are good speakers or people who don't cheat and are bad speakers?
5. Are you sure what you saw?
6. Was everyone else cheating? Has he ever cheated before?

Authority. "My teacher says the president is a good speaker." This is an appeal to authority. Is it justified in this instance?

1. What kind of speaking? Campaign? TV? State of Union?
2. What does "good" mean? Getting votes? Getting Congress to agree? Pleasing the TV commentators?
3. Authority implies that the person is an expert in the matter under discussion.
4. Can you give an example? Have all his speeches been good?
5. What teacher? Biology instructor?
6. Are the speeches really the president's, or are they written for him?

Bandwagon. "I'm glad we have a speech class. Everyone wants a speech class." Everyone is doing it so it must be good.

1. What speech classes are they taking? Discussion?
2. Who is everyone? How many?
3. Bandwagon implies that you should do what everyone else is doing.
4. Is the number of people taking the classes increasing or decreas-

ing? What about those who don't take a speech class? Can they find happiness?
5. How do you know everyone is doing it?
6. Why are they taking it? Is it an "easy A" class? Is it enjoyable?

Tradition. "If everyone else had to take speech then all the others should take it too." An appeal to tradition is based on how something was done before. "We've always done it that way."
1. Who is everyone else?
2. Why me?
3. Tradition implies that benefits accrued to people in the past and if you do the same thing now you will derive the same rewards.
4. A particular class or any class? Did some people before not take a class?
5. Who decided on this policy?
6. Are things the same as they were then, or have conditions changed?

TESTING EVIDENCE. *Fact.* The diagram may also be used to determine what is required for acceptable factual statements. A fact is the most precise statement you can make about something. Presumably, everyone would agree with the statement if they were to observe it firsthand and had the necessary expertise. Look at the statement, "The president took a speech class."
1. The President.
2. What kind of speech class?
3. A fact implies that it is a very accurate statement of some event.
4. What school did he attend? When?
5. Who was his teacher?
6. What is the source of information? Did he attend class? Did he give speeches? Did he pass the course?

Statistic. Now let's examine a statistical claim. The same type of criteria apply. The difference is primarily that a statistical statement summarizes a large number of specific facts. "Sixty four percent of successful people say a speech class helped them."
1. What is your definition of successful?
2. What is the definition of helpful?
3. Statistics generalize from a large number of events.
4. How large was the sample of events measured? Is the percentage

significant?
5. Who designed the questionnaire?
6. What were the exact questions? When? Where? Anonymous? etc.

Good listeners in an audience will justifiably take the position that if the speaker does not reveal their sources he or she has something to hide. Either the speaker is trying to take credit for ideas which are not his or her own, or the ideas came from questionable sources.

When you are trying to establish a point, your assertions must be based on reasoning that is acceptable to others. Your evidence must be based on criteria generally accepted by others.

In your speech you begin with some common ground, and then you move from one argument to another, then another, then another, and end asking for a new level of agreement that you have worked to achieve. The range of speeches called argumentative covers those that attempt to support on-going trends as well as those that try to reverse or stop a trend.

Action speech. A speech that calls for action is quite different from the speech of argument. You are trying to get people to act on what they already have chosen or agreed to, thus you may ethically include indirect suggestions and emotion. Since a listener can't take action at that moment, you are asking them to make a mental commitment. Values are important, concepts are useful, evidence helps, but the dominant element in such a speech is illustration. The listener has to be able to visualize procedures and visualize results.

Members of the audience may not know how to begin, what steps should be taken, or they may be reluctant to follow through. Resistance, habit, or timidity, must be overcome. The speech is non-controversial and may either incite an audience to act or to refrain from action.

Whereas the argument speech is a direct approach, the action speech may be indirect. The audience becomes attracted to certain behavior because it appears to fit their self-image.

For instance, about half of all United States citizens do not vote. They value democracy, they have knowledge about the candidates/issues, they have attitudes for or against the choices on the ballot – but do not act. The function of an action speech is to make a behavior appear so attractive and so important to the audience that they want to do it. While some actions are the result of deliberate decisions, many are not. The famous Russian psychologist Luria, discovered

> ...voluntary behavior is the ability to create stimuli and to subordinate them. The chief problem of all our experiments is the proof of the fundamental law: direct attempts to control his behavior always lead to negative results; its mastery is achieved only by indirect means.[1]

Much (if not all) behavioral change, habit formation, and control of skilled movement is controlled indirectly. And what is true of an individual's voluntary action may also be largely true of a person's attitudes.

> The prediction that a persuasion-induced scale shift for one attitude issue will mediate indirect attitude change toward issues sharing a comparable reference scale was supported in two experiments. Not only was indirect change produced by shifts in psychological perspective, but the magnitude of indirect change was actually greater than the magnitude of direct change.[2]

The indirect approach to influencing others also has philosophical and religious foundations.

> Kierkegaard's edifying discourse achieves its purpose by indirection and ambiguity so that if listeners are to learn anything, they have to discover it themselves.[3]

Indirect communication is actually the preferred mode in some cultures. Take for example, Japan.

> ...the Japanese have found it advisable to avoid open confrontations. Varying positions are not sharply outlined and their differences analyzed and clarified. Instead each participant in a discussion feels his way cautiously, only unfolding his own views as he sees how others react to them. Much is suggested by indirection or vague implication.
>
> Generally the Japanese, with their suspicion of verbal skills, their confidence in nonverbal understanding, their desire for consensus decisions, and their eagerness to avoid personal confrontation, do a great deal more beating around the verbal bush than we do and usually try to avoid the "frankly speaking" approach so dear to Americans. They prefer in their writing as well as their talk a loose structure of argument, rather than careful logical reasoning, and suggestion or illustration,

rather than sharp, clear statements.[4]

Motivation is best described by systems theory. New models of human behavior look at the complex interaction between the person and the action.

> In motivation theory, our attention is shifting from the enticement of eternal rewards to the intrinsic motivators that spring from the work itself. We are refocusing on the deep longings we have for community, meaning, dignity, and love in our organizational lives. We are beginning to look at the strong emotions that are part of being human, rather than segmenting ourselves (love is for home, discipline is for work) or believing that we can confine workers into narrow roles, as though they were cogs in the machinery of production. As we let go of the machine models of work, we begin to step back and see ourselves in new ways, to appreciate our wholeness....[5]

Probably the best description of this new approach is Motivational Systems Theory: Motivation = Goals x Emotions x Personal Agency Beliefs.[6]

In summary, that which is most meaningful to a person is most motivating to that person.

> We instinctively reach out to leaders who work with us on creating meaning. Those who give voice and form to our search for meaning, and who help us make our work purposeful, are leaders we cherish, and to whom we return gift for gift.[7]

The power of images. You may be aware that great religious leaders Jesus, Buddha, Lao-tze, Confucius, etc. chose parables and paradoxical sayings as their medium of teaching. Their approach was often indirect, but their effectiveness is evidenced by the large number of their followers.

> He (Buddha) deliberately withheld the knowledge He had, in order that there should be no risk after His death of followers being able to acquire information that would have no matching experience. There is nothing more productive of dissension than attempts to describe the deepest spiritual truths and experiences to those who have not themselves experienced them. For they cannot otherwise be properly understood, and will inevitably be distorted to suit the hearer's particular degree of comprehension.

> A policy of withholding or disguising the deepest spiritual truths must be followed by every spiritual reformer if he is to avoid the dissension and strife that follow the different understandings of doctrine. Without experience, an affirmation of certainty is worthless; with experience, it needs no emphasis.[8]

Don't forget there is a private part of your personality that you don't often reveal. That private domain consists largely of images: daydreams, hopes, fears, etc. We have mental pictures of ourselves doing things. And that is the province of the action speech.

> ...it is obvious that a major feature of what we view as our "personalities" derives from a set of private self-communications, interior monologues, and sequences of images, reminiscent or future-oriented, which we typically call daydreams or fantasies. The thought stream thus represents a special and important part of how we define ourselves as human beings.[9]

Describe all the physical, social, intellectual or any other implications that you can think of and then cast them in pictures that will fit the self-images of members of the audience.

Actions are described in imagery. Benefits are shown in imagery. Memories of pleasure or success are recalled in imagery. Future goals are shaped in imagery.

> ... By the age of 17 or 18, most young persons in our society are fully grown, sexually mature, and have reached the peak of their intellectual capacities for abstract thought, memory, and the other variables assessed by intelligence testing. It is no wonder, then, that the human capacity for daydreaming, for exploring the range of the "possible" through private imagery, reaches its peak in this period.[10]

Imagination is normal, frequent, powerful and consists largely of imagery.

> Our results, we believe, make it clear that sets of private intentions and motivational hierarchies as well as general and specific daydream patterns are predictive of overt behavior.[11]

Generally, imagery is more powerful than logic in changing behavior.

> ...it has been well documented that concrete, vivid images have a much stronger impact on intentions and actions than

do abstract verbal representations, even when these abstract representations logically convey much more information.[12]

This speech is for people who are already in agreement with you, so be positive and enthusiastic in your delivery. Many action speeches sound like an advertising commercial. But others may emphasize implementation in order to get a higher level of response from people. Spelling out easy steps in a practical plan may make the difference. Here are frequent components of an action speech.

Speak in personal terms.
Speak in action words.
Use word pictures.
Emphasize vivid detail.
Use metaphor and comparison.
Use positive statements.
Use repetition, rhyme, and rhythm.
Describe goals and future possibilities.
Describe feelings and emotions.
Create imaginary scenes.
Use humor, if appropriate.
State your personal commitment.

Speech purpose adaptation. The four idealized speech models illustrate principles and strategies for idealized audiences. Sometimes your material applies well to some members in your audience, but not all of them. Another time you may want to direct your speech to people not in your immediate audience. And a third occasion is when you have to cover more than one purpose to be successful.

Portion-of-the-audience. In this situation you find your speech material is excellent for a large number in the audience, but not to everyone. When you give this type of speech you should announce what you are doing so those who are not directly spoken to are acknowledged. "I would like to talk primarily to those who are prospective teachers, but the rest of you will be interested...." "You men need to know how we women...."

Absentee audience. Here you have a challenge or advice for a group that is not present in your audience. Your audience however, benefits from what you say. Perhaps you are figuratively telling Congress what laws should be passed, or alcoholics what they should do.

Republicans criticize Democrats at Republican gatherings and even ministers admonish from the pulpit those who don't attend church. These speeches still serve valuable purposes, they reinforce the conviction and commitment of your audience who later may encounter individuals from the other group. This has been called an "inoculation" speech.

Multiple purpose. This speech fits an occasion where you want to inform, but have to increase audience awareness first. Or, in order to elicit action you have to eliminate alternative choices. You may recognize that in your audience there are people who are in each of the different stages of decision making and you have to address some appropriate remarks to each of them.

If you wanted to cover all four purposes, in the first part of your speech (awareness) you might explain why the subject is important. In the second part (information) you could review the important ideas (which may be new to some people). Then you could make a recommendation (argument) and answer any possible objections that you think the audience might have. And finally, you might suggest what action should be taken. This speech obviously would require more time to present.

You try to help those who are not aware to become so, you give solid information to those who are seeking it, you evaluate alternatives and recommend a choice to those who are trying to decide what is best, and you describe procedures making action easier for those who delay.

It's not likely that you could make everyone in your audience equally aware, equally informed, equally in favor of a policy, and equally committed to an action. But it's also reasonable that you could make some changes for different individuals depending on their state of readiness. After your speech one listener may have been alerted, another informed, another made a choice, and yet another has resolved to take some action. So you may have maximized the amount of change for the greatest number of people in a general audience even though different people drew different messages from your speech.

There is no simple formula which persuades or motivates all people. Different people change their priorities, beliefs, attitudes, and behaviors for different reasons.

However, there is a powerful constant, and that is focusing on the personal relationship. In research on the effectiveness of different therapies the evidence suggests that they all work, but the effectiveness differs not so much because of the theoretical approach, but more on the basis of the relationship, specifically: accurate empathy, non-possessive warmth, and genuiness.[13] Thus, the perceived relationship is at least equal to the content of the speech in producing change.

Idea Patterns. Textbooks in both English and communication commonly list around 12 to 15 organizational patterns. If you analyze the structures you see that basically ideas are related to each other in only two ways: serial and parallel – sequence and correlation. Then there is a non-pattern which is a list of ideas without either sequence or correlation (topical, etc.). It's not surprising that the two patterns reflect how the brain processes information.

Idea-imagery outline. This outline does not dictate structure, but instead reveals the natural relationships between ideas. It also facillitates creativity in arrangement. It does not make decisions for you, but separates your material so you can see all the patterns that exist. The ideas may be arranged in any order, deductive or inductive.

Idea statements may come first and organize or group together other idea statements.

Main idea- Team sports are overemphasized in universities.
Idea- 1. University sports should follow the ancient Greek model.
Idea- 2. Life-time sports have more educational value.

Idea statements may also be used to group together imagery statements.

Main idea- U.S. courts protect human rights.
Imagery- 1. My personal experience in court.
Imagery- 2. Court procedures in Russia.

But a speaker may also present imagery first and use that to organize or group together idea statements. In that instance the ideas support or emphasize important parts of the description or action.

Main imagery- Story of the moonshot.
Idea- 1. This illustrates cooperation between scientists.

Idea- 2. Government can provide leadership for private industry.

And imagery can be used to organize or bring together other imagery.

Main imagery- Description of a factory emitting pollutants.
Imagery- 1. Description of effects on beaches.
Imagery- 2. Description of effects on wildlife.

The idea-first pattern is most common because students have been taught to organize speeches with a logical outline where imagery material is presented after each idea is stated.

You could, however, organize a speech as a series of illustrations or evidence and make a conclusion or main point after each one. It is equally effective and sometimes a speaker finds it easier to remember a speech which is a series of word pictures as opposed to a speech consisting of logical statements.

First, you start by asking, what are the relationships between the ideas that you want to include in your speech? Do you see any natural progressions of time or place or logic? Do you see any ideas that pair off with other ideas because of similarity or contrast? Do you find a list of ideas without any sequence or correlation?

Second, you check whether you have some imagery for each main idea.

Third, you decide whether you want the idea or the imagery to lead-come first.

Speech format plan. The concept of a beginning and ending which is separate from the main part of a message is unique to a speech.

Introduction. Its function is not to get "attention." Emphasis on attention at the beginning of a speech is the *least* important place. Telling jokes, or using some gimmick at the beginning is unnecessary, and often counter-productive. Even Aristotle recognized this principle.

> Again, the business of exciting attention is common to all the divisions of a speech wherever it may be necessary; for the audience relax their attention anywhere rather than at the beginning, when more particularly everyone is at the summit of attention.[14]

The beginning of a speech does not have to be sensationalized like the beginning of articles, because for the first few seconds you have a captive audience. You do however, have to seize that advantage and direct the attention to important material, in order to keep it.

The function of the opening lines of a speech is to *unify.* You want the audience to sense a relationship between you and them.

There are three common errors made by poor speakers. First, their beginning is too long. Sometimes they think of several different ways to start their speech, and then use all of them. If this is your tendency, you might want to limit your beginning to one sentence, so you don't ramble.

Second, they believe they have to be funny. This is seen by the audience as artificial because that beginning joke is the only place in their speech where there is any humor. Don't try to be funny if it is not completely natural to you, and only use humor directly related to your subject.

The third mistake is their beginning has a negative tone. Don't call attention to your nervousness, or describe how much trouble you had preparing the speech. Don't make apologies or give excuses, no matter how true they may be!

To determine what you should say in your beginning, ask yourself these questions. Do you need to be introduced to the audience? If so, introduce yourself. Is there something about your *approach* that needs an introduction? If it is a little unusual, or you want a fair hearing, you may need to prepare the audience. Do they need information about the events that brought you to this *occasion*? Perhaps you have just recently come to the point of view that you are now advocating. Does the *source* of your information need to be introduced? Maybe the audience is not aware of how authoritative your particular source is. In other words, anything the audience needs to know before you begin your message should be explained at the beginning.

Some textbooks list different types of content that can be used for introductions – in actuality, *there isn't anything you can't use!* The purpose is to bring the wandering thoughts of people in the audience to a sharp focus on your message. You want to unite their thoughts with your thoughts and when they are mentally with you, you start your message.

Preview. A preview announces the ideas to be discussed or the purpose of the speech. Explicit structure helps the audience both to follow you as you speak, and to remember your ideas afterward. Sometimes the wording of your preview becomes a theme, motto, slogan, or phrase that can be repeated for emphasis throughout the speech.

There are a few special cases when a preview is not used, but remember they are exceptions. If you have a speech that develops to a climax, and if revealing the end beforehand would spoil the effect, then you wouldn't use the preview. If you have a surprise argument, you may want to spring it after you have built a foundation for it. One other case is when the emphasis is on imagery rather than ideas. Then, the preview is unnecessary.

Message. The most common mistake made in the body of the speech is the assumption that an audience can follow the organizational pattern without help, but the speaking situation requires a lot of organizational statements and a lot of repetition.

Transitions. They include statements of the speaker's intention (now I want to discuss....), purpose (I feel that we should all....), and motivation (the reason I'm telling you these things, is....). They emphasize (this is really important....) or enumerate (third,....) the order of thoughts in your speech.

Transitions need to stand out like flags on a golf course. Otherwise the audience's attention may wander off course. *In contrast, you'll almost never find these techniques used in magazine articles, newspapers, or other writing.*

> But to write with economy as well as clarity, he (the writer) must eventually learn that in closely knit paragraphs transitions are often invisible. ... If his argument is firmly constructed, the transitions will usually take care of themselves.[15]

The bias in writing is to create a smooth flow of thoughts. And techniques like previews, prominent transitions, and reviews would interrupt that flow. So if you copy an article for your speech, you'll probably be missing those structural aids which are crucial to oral communication.

Ideas. Ideas consist of assertions or claims you make, the reasoning in your speech, the logical argument, the persuasive suggestion, or the hypothesis you advance. Those statements indicate what you think, feel, want, believe, hope, etc.

Imagery. Imagery is divided for convenience into two categories, evidence and illustration – but the difference is one of degree. Illustrations are ordinary examples that may be actual or imaginary, but evidence is the most accurate kind of statement that you can make about something. Examples, anecdotes, analogies, stories, jokes, and most quotations may be called illustrations. A quote from someone who is an authority about something you are trying to prove, however, would be evidence.

Evidence has the backing of well-established, credible sources and is stated with precision. Descriptions of time (June 6), place (Vancouver, B.C.), degree (the fourth highest), quantity (39%), etc. are required.

Your personal observations are illustrations in most cases, but could be expert testimony in an area where you have considerable experience. It's important that the audience know about your expertise however, because ultimately evidence rests on a belief in the accuracy of the information.

Review. A review reflects back to your preview. If you listed your main points then you could summarize them. If you stated your purpose or introduced a theme then you could repeat it again. It provides another repetition before ending.

Conclusion. The primary problem with most endings is that they are too abrupt. As you near the end you should signal the audience to pay attention to your final sentences – you do that with a pause. Ending sentences, like the beginning, should also create unity. They restate the agreements you feel you have achieved. Often, only a couple of sentences are sufficient. A well-organized speech keeps the central thoughts clear throughout and leads to a verdict which can be simply stated, but with emphasis.

The ending can refer back to the beginning. If you began with a question, you could end with the answer. If you began with a startling statement you could repeat the same statement at the end and the audience would have a new understanding of what you meant. Encapsulate your message in words that will be memorable to the audience.

Language plan. Language patterns are powerful in shaping your speaker-audience relationship.

Pronunciation and grammar. A decision on effective use of language is a choice between, 1) those words and/or pronunciations which are a part of your natural vocabulary, and 2) those words and/or pronunciations which are preferred because the dictionaries confirm their wide-spread use. Written material is judged exclusively by the second standard, but spoken English allows for modification of the conventions due to the immediacy of the situation. If you know that you and your audience share the same specific language patterns there is no risk, but if your audience has people from different backgrounds, then there will be some who expect widely accepted standards.

The *general risk* is that those in your audience who know conventional usage will be surprised if you don't use those forms. The *specific risk* is that those in your audience who don't know the conventional usage will be surprised if you don't speak the same way they do.

An audience compares their knowledge with your knowledge. If your language sounds different, they wonder if your knowledge is as good as their knowledge. Using the correct pronunciation of a word leads the audience to believe that you have expertise in the subject matter. If you say you like to read "po ems" (two syllables) many people will believe you know something about poetry. But if you pronounce it as one syllable, some people will consider your knowledge as limited.

When describing functions of the government, will the audience accept your ideas as easily if you don't say "gov ern ment" (three syllables)? The criticism may be extremely unfair, but you want to eliminate any possible criticism. If you say "li berry" instead of "li brary" some individuals might question if you have ever been in one. And while they may accept you as a person, they might not accept your opinions or recommendations.

Using the pronunciation preferred by the majority of educated people implies that you have benefited from exposure to a wide range of ideas and people from many backgrounds. This leads your audience to believe your conclusions are based on considerable information and you are not narrow in your thinking.

Now that may not be true at all, but an audience doesn't have much to go on to decide whether they believe you, so they'll use whatever they can. If you say "ath a lete" instead of "ath lete" people may conclude that all you know about a sport is how to play the game and there may be more important issues that you want to discuss. Don't pronounce the w in "towards" or the t in "often" and you'll gain credibility.

Are you aware that words used as both nouns and verbs have a shift in the accented syllable? The noun is stressed on the first syllable but a verb usage moves the emphasis to the last syllable.

NOUN-VERB STRESS SHIFT

Noun	Verb
Ob' ject	Ob ject'
In' crease	In crease'
Dis' count	Dis count'

This is a list of words often mispronounced by placing the stress on the wrong syllable.

PRONUNCIATION OF SELECTED WORDS

First syllable stress		Second syllable stress	
Ad' mirable	Com' parable	Irrev' ocable	Cement'
Ap' plicable	Fav' orite	Insur' ance	Enthus' iasm
Gen' uine	In' dustry	Finan' ce	Inquir' y
In' teresting	Pos' itively	Preten' se	Resear' ch
Pref' erable	The' ater	Super' flous	Routine'

Also, some very different words sound very much alike unless you pronounce them very clearly.

EASILY CONFUSED WORDS

Word	Meaning	Word	Meaning
Accept	to receive	Inequity	unfairness
Except	to exclude	Iniquity	sin
Adapt	to suit to	Interment	burial
Adept	proficient	Internment	detention
Digression	deviations	Parcel	a piece
Discretion	judgment	Partial	part of
Dissolution	termination	Persecute	harm
Disillusion	remove false impression	Prosecute	law suit
Elicit	to draw out	Perspective	view

Illicit	illegal	Prospective	expected
Exceed	to surpass	Precede	go before
Accede	to agree	Proceed	to begin
Formally	ceremonious	Commuted	substitute less
Formerly	in times past	Computed	calculation

1) If you can, check out the language patterns of your audience, 2) learn what the accepted forms are, 3) develop a sensitivity to word usage.

Explanation or description. These categories contrast a logical style with an imaginative style. Those are the two basic ways of teaching, learning, thinking, and problem solving. We use the processes of both hemispheres in everything we do, but there are good reasons to sometimes emphasize one style more than the other.

Explanation, typically, is a more rational, analytic approach. It names things and tells about its components. It's perhaps the most common type of expression. Description on the other hand, tends to emphasize sensory detail, evokes feelings with the pictures it presents, and is usually more colorful. Contrast the language that a botanist might use to explain the biological structures and processes of a flower with the words of a poet describing that same flower. Explanation uses neutral language and description uses strong language.

Slang and definition. Slang is a problem because it varies from year to year, and place to place. Not all the people in an audience will know what various slang terms mean. So, if you want to use a powerful slang expression, make sure that the audience can tell by the context what it means – or else define it. Another difficulty with slang is that it is over-used. That is, when the same expression is used over and over and over and over again, it loses forcefulness. Because it may be misunderstood by some, and be boring to others, you often have as much to lose as you have to gain by using slang.

Define all unfamiliar or technical terms.

Humor. If you are naturally humorous it is a great asset, but if you tell jokes because you think you should, you've made a mistake.

A joke at the beginning of a speech can backfire for two reasons. It can fall flat and that creates a new barrier to overcome, but it can also be so funny that the audience keeps on laughing while you move on to other ideas – that's even worse. If the audience is mentally repeating the joke to themselves so they can remember it later, you've lost them. So your attempt to gain attention was a failure, their attention is on the joke and not on your message.

The solution is to use that sense of humor which is naturally yours. If you know a clever story or joke that relates directly to your subject, then of course you should use it. And if you're one of those fortunate individuals who has a talent for humorous expression then you should use that skill throughout your speech.

Figures of speech. "Figures of speech" are very impressive ways of communicating and are powerful in arousing feelings. Most figures of speech are created by either comparison or repetition (correlation process). Following is a list of figures of speech that are based on metaphor. Note the variety of ways that comparisons can be made.

FIGURES OF SPEECH BASED ON COMPARISON

Referring to a person, idea or event in a casual way – *allusion*
Substituting a proper name for a common name – *antonomasia*
Representing the size of the object by the size of the word – *bulk*
An apparent congruity but an actual incongruity – *bull*
Naming a thing in a round-about way – *circumlocution*
Substituting one expression for another – *correction*
Substituting one part of speech for another – *enallage*
Collapsed metaphor used as an adjective – *epithet*
Substituting an inoffensive word for an offensive word – *euphemism*
Dividing what is really a unity – *hendidays*
Substituting words which are opposite to the meaning intended – *irony*
Substituting a characteristic for the name of the thing itself – *kenning*
Substituting an attribute for the name of the thing itself – *metonymy*
Imitation of the sound of the thing or action – *onomatopeia*
The union of contradictory terms – *oxymoron*
Attributing life to inanimate objects or abstractions – *personification*
Direct comparison using "like" or "as" – *simile*
A part is substituted for the whole or the whole for a part – *synecdoche*
Implied comparison – *trope*

Yoking two words to another word that doesn't apply equally – *zeugma*

Comparisons of sound, word, or thought can be powerful and beautiful. Still other figures of speech are based on rhythm and rhyme. Notice how many figures of speech are based on repetition of words.

FIGURES OF SPEECH BASED ON REPETITION

Repeat word at beginning of one clause and end of another – *anadiplosis*
Repetition of word at beginning of successive clauses – *anaphora*
Repetition of word at end of successive clauses – *conversion*
Repeat same word at beginning and end of sentence – *epidiplosis*
Immediate repetition of the same emphatic word – *gemination*
Repetition of the same word in a different sense – *ploce*
Repeat ideas in reverse order – *chiasmus*
Repeat word at beginning and end of successive clauses – *symploce*
Repetition of same sound at beginning – *alliteration*
Repetition of similar vowel within words – *assonance*
Repetition of final consonant – *consonance*
Repetition of sound – *echo*
Repetitive use of "neithers" and "nors" – *paradiastole*
Pairing similar ideas by repetition of form – *parallelism*
Words repeat the same sound with different meaning – *pun*

The technical labels are not important, but the process of creating comparisons and rhythmic patterns in your speaking is very important. They are a natural part of language and aid a listener's comprehension and recall.

Oratory. Anciently, oratory was closely associated with stylistic concerns, like figures of speech. But consider a different conception. Oratory occurs when an audience's *own experience* speaks to them in the unmistakably clear words which are framed by the speaker and resonate within them. Frye has used these phrases to describe the event.

> ...style rises from communication to community, and achieves a vision of society which draws speaker and hearer together into a closer bond. It is the voice of the genuine individual reminding us of our genuine selves, and of our role as

> members of a society, in contrast to a mob. Such style has a peculiar quality of penetration about it: it elicits a shock of recognition, as it is called, which is the proof of the genuiness.[16]

That usually happens when a speaker finds a new expression or unique way of saying something as opposed to the usual, common phrases that we've all heard. It happens when a speaker shares a very personal feeling which relates to reactions we have also been experiencing. That expression describes powerfully or beautifully what we've felt, but only faintly recognized, and haven't been able to put it in words. The speaker is able to describe what we haven't been able to identify, to clarify our own feelings, to express clearly our desires which have been fuzzy, to articulate goals we've been unable to define. At those times the speaker communicates across social differences.

Your words are given meaning by the audience because of their own experiences which arouse in them feelings similar to your own. Among the many levels where thoughts and feelings are exchanged, you sometimes find a "window" where a message sails through undistorted to strike the same chords of human experience. That experience occurs when the speaker-audience relationship is authentic. That's when you are being as honest as you know how and are trying to understand the real experience of your audience.

Oratory emerges from integrity, empathy, and creativity. The words and delivery of the speaker are synchronized in a way that effectively matches the thoughts of the audience on an important subject and touches them deeply.

Delivery plan. Now that you have organized your content and made decisions about your language choices you are ready to develop a plan for the delivery of your speech.

Maintaining audience attention requires variety and if you don't plan to have variety, you probably won't have any. Some people have a mistaken notion that talking loudly will hold attention, or that talking fast will hold attention. *Physiologically, you cannot sustain any emotion at a high level for an extended period of time.* In order to maintain a focus on an idea you must have a series of builds.

Sequence. Your delivery plan grows out of your content plan. In a progression pattern the points of the speech are emphasized so that each point is a little stronger than the one before which carries along the feeling. Or, instead of increasing in intensity you can start with a strong emphasis and then reduce it in a fading pattern. The feeling of progression is powerful whether it is increased speed or volume, or whether it is decreasing pace and pauses.

Correlation. The pairing pattern emphasizes the important similarities or the important differences that are crucial in your message. Major comparisons are accented. Two ideas of equal importance are given the same amount of emphasis. This helps the audience feel the issues that clash or the ideas that reinforce each other.

Selection. This pattern means that you arbitraily select what you want to emphasize. Emphasis is placed on the particular ideas or imagery which are more important for the audience to remember. You match your emphasis to the significant points of your speech.

Impromptu speech. It may have any speech purpose; you could talk about a value, inform, argue, or ask for action.

The key to creative speaking is creative listening. Be alert to what people are saying and doing. Review what you have been thinking about and what other people have been saying.

For example, last night you may have had conversations with people – what did they say? What did you say? Yesterday what subjects were you talking about? Last week? Last month?

Review quickly the ideas you've heard. Recall if you agreed; if so, what's your reason? If you disagreed, what's your reason? And if you're confused, then there is something contradictory or not clear in the messages, try to identify the problem.

If focusing on the past doesn't suggest something, think about the future. What do you look forward to today? What do you expect will happen tomorrow, this week, this month? Do you like your prospects? Are you anxious about what may happen? Thinking about hopes and fears usually provokes excellent subjects.

If you pay attention to what people are saying, and form an opinion of your own, you'll always be able to ask a question, answer a question, or give an impromptu speech.

Psychologically, there are two opposite styles even though you could use a combination of them. Some people find they need a structure first, that they can fit information into. Others must think of ideas or examples first, before they can see what relationships exist and how the thoughts could be put together. Remember, your model can always be modified as necessary, it is a catalyst, not a strait-jacket. For some speakers the impromptu speech is the most difficult of all speeches to give, yet for other speakers, it is the easiest. The reason is whether the individual's strength is in organization or in delivery, whether ideas come slowly or quickly.

Part III, Chapter 16

Aiding Memory

Personal effectiveness decisions. The person who can think with pictures in their mind has an advantage, they can usually give speeches without notes.

The deductive versus inductive bias shows up again in memory strategy. One aspect is whether the emphasis is on parts or the whole.

Another aspect is how the different parts are connected – tight or loose.

The advantage here is for speakers who naturally speak out loud and move. If the other speakers can learn this technique they will benefit greatly from it.

The number of times a speech should be rehearsed is very personal – each speaker must find that out for themselves.

Obviously, if a speaker can speak without notes they have a great advantage. However, other speakers can learn to use notes unobtrusively.

Myth of rote rehearsal. This myth is that memory is improved by rote repetition. Some speakers believe that the more times they go over a speech the better they will remember it. However, word-for-word repeating is a booby-trap, because if you don't remember every word exactly in the right order you won't be able to continue. Improving memory is not a quantitative process, it is qualitative. A few creative rehearsals serve you better than hours of repetition. Consider the following research conclusions.

1. A "single retrieval path" is not as efficient as "multiple retrieval paths."[1]
2. People who actively visualize (drawing) and verbalize (talking) remember better than people who do not.[2]
3. Organized rehearsal is a necessary condition for organized recall.[3]
4. Elaborative rehearsal is superior to maintenance rehearsal.[4]
5. Words which provoke high imagery are remembered better than words that have low imagery value.[5]
6. Even imagery words are not remembered as well if they lack a context.[6]
7. A strong rehearsal the night before you speak is better than a rehearsal the morning of the day you speak.[7]
8. Just prior to speaking, a low arousal rehearsal is more beneficial, but a few days beforehand you should have vigorous rehearsals.[8]
9. Material is best recalled when you are at the same level of arousal as when the material was learned.[9]

The alternative is idea plus imagery in a context. Associations should be created which combine abstract ideas with concrete imagery in a context (organization).

For example, Jayne[10] measured the recall of words in a poem and found that the beginning words, the ending words, and unusual words had high recall (idea features). He also found that words related to pictures, metaphors, and rhymes had high recall (imagery features). These two features combine the cognitive processes of the two brain hemispheres.

If your preparation has followed the steps previously described, look at what you already have in your favor.

1. If your main ideas were formed after reflective thought then they are *yours* and will be easier to recall than if you had copied the ideas of someone else.
2. If you have put your ideas in the simple *speech format* they will be easier to recall than if they were in the complex structure of written material.
   A. A speech format calls for a *few* ideas, not many like you find in articles.
   B. A speech format calls for prominent *transitions* between ideas, which helps memory. You can even give numbers to the ideas to make them stand out.

C. A speech format calls for *repetition* of the ideas in a preview and review. Those summaries reinforce each other and facilitate recall.

3. If you have *matched* ideas to imagery the *combination* produces a strong memory bond.
4. If you have planned your own *content pattern* it will be easier to remember than someone else's organizational pattern.
5. If your ideas are in the *speaking idiom* you'll remember them better. The vocabulary is simpler, the structure of sentences is simpler. But above all, those are your words.
6. If you have created a *delivery plan* you have a pattern of meaningful emphasis to reinforce your recall.
7. Now, you can use *planned rehearsals* to build a memory chain that links together all those different aspects of your speech.

Some parts are easier to remember than others. The beginning sentences are the easiest part of the entire speech to remember because just prior to speaking you can read them over several times. That puts you into your speech with an effective start.

The ending statements should also be written down in the exact words you have chosen. When you arrive at the end of your speech, look down at those sentences, then look up and repeat them with confidence that they clearly state what you want to say.

And you don't really need to memorize quotes or statistics or facts. Evidence can be written down and read from cards at the appropriate time during the speech. Illustrations, like stories or examples, actually are quite easy to remember. But it's appropriate to read them also if necessary. So the imagery in your speech is not much of a memory problem. That leaves only the main ideas that really have to be learned.

MEMORY TASK

Beginning sentences (Written down)

Ideas (Learn)	Imagery (Written down)

Ending sentences (Written down)

Conversational style. Conversational style refers to language, to idea organization, and delivery.

A conversational style will be facilitated by the speech format, by the speaking idiom, and by variety in delivery. "It takes a lot of practice to sound natural."[11]

Delivery notes. A professional speaker should know how to work from no notes, or brief notes, or how to write a script and read it effectively. Some situations do call for a speech to be read. But there are other occasions when a script would get in your way. If you want to move around, show visual aids, or make a very strong point, for example, even notes could prevent you from being effective.

It doesn't matter whether you have the speech memorized, or are reading a speech, *what matters is how you sound and appear to the audience.* Whether you use scripts or notes, the question is how well you use them. They are only an aid to memory, not a substitute for it.

If the situation doesn't dictate it, then *your choice of memory technique should be made on the basis of your thinking style.* Some people's memory is more visual, others is more auditory, some are even kinesthetic. Some people can easily elaborate on a few ideas. Other people are better at reducing many thoughts down to a few. Instead of thinking about "memorizing," think about "learning."

When working from a script the biggest problem you face is that after you look up from the page you may lose your place when you look down again. But there is a simple solution, *begin each sentence at the left margin of the page.* That way you can always look down the left side of your page and quickly find the next sentence.

When rehearsing, search for opportunities to look up from the page to make eye-contact with your audience.

Your beginning can be given while looking at your audience.

Your ending can be given with full eye-contact.

Your transitional sentences are easy to remember and don't need to be read.

Stories, examples, and other imagery probably don't need to be read.

Any ordinary sentence with ordinary wording you can probably remember.

You can look up at the end of your sentences.

Don't practice using the script, practice <u>not</u> using it! As you rehearse more and more with a memory aid you use it less and less. Don't train yourself to use it, practice not using it. That is the key principle in rehearsals.

A preparation outline served the purpose of organizing your material and its structure was dictated by that purpose. Now you want notes to serve a different purpose – to aid your memory – so its structure is different.

You only need those words, phrases, or sentences that serve as memory cues. You should tailor it to suit your personal memory requirements. Write down all that you need to help you recall your ideas, but don't write any more than you need. And the spacing you use serves to make it 1) easy to read, and 2) easy to make changes, if necessary.

Notes may be written either on cards or paper, it's your choice. The advantage of cards is that they don't make any noise when you move them and being small in size they are not as noticeable. The advantage of paper is that you don't need many sheets, perhaps only one, and that eliminates turning or moving something. You don't want either distracting sounds or distracting movements.

Some people tend to over-rehearse. They don't feel that it is possible to practice too much. Others deliberately under-rehearse, because they're afraid that too much rehearsal will ruin the delivery. If content, organization, and written language skills are your strengths, more rehearsals give a sense of security. But if your strengths are in spontaneous expression, being a little underprepared will give a quality of immediacy.

Combining the two brain hemisphere functions unites the full capacity of the brain to recall your message.

> ...Brenda Milner...has examined an easy memory task that relies on activities of two systems, one in each hemisphere. Subjects were shown twenty-five simple drawings that could be remembered both as words and as visual images. Damage to one temporal lobe had little effect on immediate recall of the pictures. But the next day, subjects with either right or left temporal damage showed..."a whopping drop" in ability to remember the pictures.[12]

Those people had the effective use of only one hemisphere which means they could remember either a word or a picture. In the short run they did as well as anyone. But the following day their memory loss was dramatic.

A similar finding was noted for people who received electroshock.[13] When the left hemisphere received the shock the person could not remember words, but could remember different objects. And when the right received the shock that same person could not remember any of those objects, but could remember the words they were shown.

To remember ideas you relate them to imagery, and to remember imagery you relate them to ideas. That's why this text suggested from the very beginning that the best way to get a subject is to view a speech as a collection of ideas and imagery and the best way to organize the material is according to ideas and imagery relationships.

Can you think in pictures? Then use imagery as your main organization pattern for memory. If you think primarily in words, use your ideas as the main organization pattern for your speech.

Visual aid(s). An entire speech can be organized around visuals of some kind. However, they require more rehearsal time to integrate them into your speech.

Visual aids are *organizational* aids. They make complex information easier to understand; pictures show relationships between points quickly and charts can reduce large amounts of data to a single perception. That saves you time.

A visual aid improves *memory.* A large poster for the audience to see may be the actual outline of your speech. You look at the poster along with the audience and expand on the statements. Or, you may hold a poster in front of you that has your speech outline written on the back. A visual aid also serves as a memory aid for the audience; a picture, diagram or sentence that depicts your speech nucleus or your main points can help the audience remember what you want them to recall.

Visual aids provide *emphasis,* they center attention and focus interest. They give variety to a presentation in the same way that movement, gesture, and vocal change emphasize your main points.

Limitations. But there are also possible disadvantages if they: can't be clearly seen, take too much time, or overpower the message. To use visual aids plan carefully the size, the physical placement, and the timing. Sometimes a visual aid takes too much time to demonstrate or manipulate – then don't use it. Some visuals overwhelm the content.

Even the clothes you wear are visual aids which support or detract from a speech.

Mark in your notes exactly when you will pick up the aid and reveal it to the audience. Don't show an aid until you are ready to talk about it. Then, don't talk to the aid; merely glance at the aid, but face and speak to the audience. Then remove the aid or cover it before you talk about the next point in your speech.

Only rarely would you pass out something at the beginning of your speech, because it would detract from what you're saying unless it's very simple.

Visual aids for numbers. This is a situation where a visual aid is critical – but use the right kind. Certain charts show some information better than others; in fact a chart can be misleading or inaccurate if data is placed in the wrong format.

The first question you ask is: do my numbers describe something that occurred over a period of time or at one moment in time? If you have data reflecting a time series then you use a line or column chart. If your data came from a measurement taken at one particular instance, then use a pie chart, 100% column chart, bar chart, or frequency distribution.

The line chart and the column chart can be used intechangeably to compare *rates* of change over a period of time.

TIME SERIES CHARTS

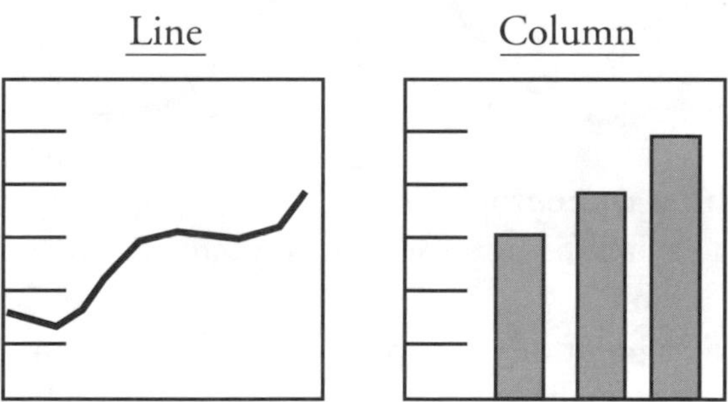

They both can compare several series of data, but each one has a particular advantage. The line better emphasizes trends that occur and the column emphasizes size or magnitude over time.

When your data are showing the *relative* magnitude of different parts of the same thing you select from a pie chart, 100% column chart, bar chart, or frequency distribution as shown below.

MAGNITUDE CHARTS

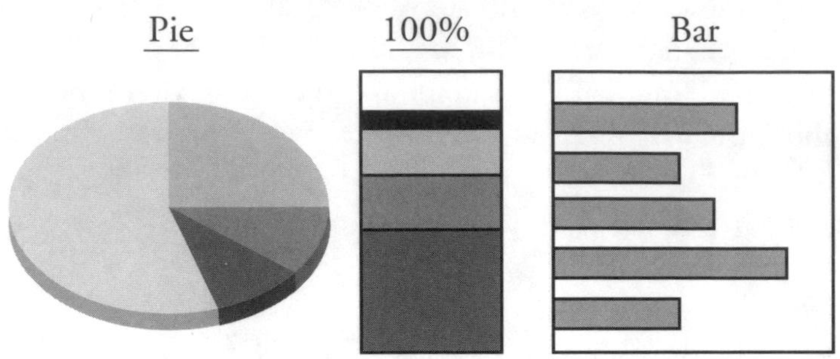

If the number of divisions of one thing you are depicting is a small number (up to about 8) you could use the pie chart or 100% column chart. The pie chart is particularly good for depicting money or budgets of one kind or another. If the number of sub-divisions is greater, then for clarity you might want to use the bar chart.

The frequency distribution is used to show the relative distribution of measures at one time and is primarily used for measures of human behavior patterns.

FREQUENCY DISTRIBUTION

Mental pictures content rehearsal. Take the points from your notes and create a mental picture for each of them which you project on the walls of a room.

For the first point of your speech, you develop a pictorial representation and mentally place it on the left side wall of the room. Imagine that you really see a picture which depicts what you want to say. Then on the far back wall, you place another image or symbol which reminds you of the second main point in your speech. You continue by creating a picture for your third major point and locating it on the side wall to your right. You place the fourth one on the wall directly behind you, the fifth one goes on the ceiling, and the sixth you put on the floor. If you have more than six ideas you could subdivide those areas. That is, you can divide a wall vertically and place a different idea on each half of the wall.

Creating visual images of things you want to remember is not a new idea, but assigning them to the walls of the room where you will be speaking is a practical adaptation for the public speaker.

Language rehearsal. Another important skill is to learn how to memorize ideas rather than words. The secret is to rehearse by going through the speech several times without repeating the same words twice. The first time through it doesn't matter what words you use for each idea or image. But the next time through you think of other words to say the same thing. For example, one time you might use long sentences and the next time you would use very short sentences. With another repetition, try colorful expressions. Then, another time use very precise language. Use active verbs, then use passive verbs, etc.

Choose a different pattern of language and use it for the entire speech each time you go through it. Force yourself to find synonyms for different words. This helps you remember ideas rather than the words.

You will not be able to go rapidly through your speech using this procedure but you do not improve memory by how fast you rehearse, or by the number of repetitions, you improve memory by creating different associations or relationships.

Then you won't be tied to one particular way of saying your ideas and thus you avoid the boobytrap of forgetting a word and not being able to continue. In fact, you'll discover that you will be able to think of different ways to phrase your ideas even while you are speaking.

When you stand to deliver your speech you will have confidence in your memory. You know that you will not forget your ideas because you have said them several different ways, plus you could even think up an entirely new way of saying your ideas because you have practiced doing that very thing.

Delivery rehearsal. Did you know that reading your speech silently to yourself will give a time measurement very different from one when you say the words aloud? The timed duration of your speech will also vary depending on whether you are sitting down or standing. Obviously, to get a close approximation of how long your speech really is, you'll need to time yourself when you are standing and saying your speech out loud.

Work from the memory aid you're actually going to use, but most importantly, speak out loud and gesture with enthusiasm. The more energetic the better – its easy to tone down your gesture or voice later. Exaggeration in rehearsal helps you increase the variety in your delivery.

But don't practice a particular gesture for a particular word or phrase. Rather, change the gestures each time you repeat your speech. You are not practicing individual gestures, you are getting used to some kind of emphasis at certain places in your speech. Those places where you want emphasis was decided when you made your delivery plan. Now follow the plan, but practice different types of delivery emphasis at those places in your speech.

Walk during this rehearsal. Get your body used to deliberate movement when certain ideas are being spoken. Try to make your body and voice more alive to the meaning of your words and ideas. Don't just pace aimlessly. Move to a particular place, state an idea, then move to another place to state another idea.

Sometimes you hit on some specific language, gesture, or vocal change that you would like to use in your presentation. That's OK, during delivery you'll note whether that specific language, gesture, or vocal change fits the audience size, audience receptivity, and the feeling you have built up to at that particular point in your speech, before you use it. So even a specific pattern you want to use should be judged "appropriate" to the circumstances or you would not use it.

In all your preparation, but particularly in your rehearsals, you not only make a plan, you also prepare to modify that plan if necessary.

Summary: the pictures you conjure up and place on the walls where you speak involve visual memory. They are then associated with the ideas of your speech which consists of verbal memory. That is finally associated with your delivery plan which is kinesthetic memory. You have formed relationships between pictures, words and actions.

Notice also that you have practiced under different conditions of emotional arousal. The content rehearsal is done mentally in a relaxed, imaginative mood. Language rehearsal is a moderate state of verbalizing different words and sentences. And the delivery rehearsal is an energetic practice with strong movement and gesture.

Lowering Stress

Personal effectiveness decisions. Most speakers tend to fidget, but some tend to freeze up. That makes a difference when the speaker is trying to cope and adapt.

Again, most speakers tend to be more aware of a rapid heartbeat, but not all, some are more aware of stomach sensations.

Most feel their skin getting warm, but some feel the opposite.

Most feel dryness in mouth, but some feel the opposite. However, it should not be assumed that fidgeting, heartbeat, warm skin and dry mouth all go together.

Public speaking instruction traditionally has emphasized content over delivery, and education in general emphasizes the deductive approach rather than the inductive, so it's probably natural that more speakers would have that bias, even though some may have more natural ability in a holistic style.

It's reassuring that almost half the speakers experience a decrease in speech stress after the first few sentences of their speeches.

Myth of stage-fright. The myth is that speaking before an audience is a "fearful" experience. The concept of stage-fright is linked to the fight-flight response discovered by Walter B. Cannon.

> It (adrenalin) cooperates with sympathetic nerve impulses thus flooding the blood with sugar; it helps in distributing the blood to the heart, lungs, central nervous system and limbs, while taking it away from the inhibited organs of the abdomen; it quickly abolishes the effects of muscular fatigue;

> and it renders the blood more rapidly coagulable. These remarkable facts are, furthermore, associated with some of the most primitive experiences in the life of higher organisms, experiences common to all, both man and beast, the elementary experiences of pain and fear and rage that come suddenly in critical emergencies.[1]

The fight-flight response is a "primitive" alarm system which we share with animals. However, speaking to an audience is not a critical emergency like suddenly coming across a bear in your path. Your anticipation of speaking is a socialized response based on knowledge of audience expectations (not primitive) and it builds slowly for days prior to the event with your last few hours or minutes seeming like forever (not an emergency). If speakers truly experienced a fight-flight reaction, then they would all have identical adrenalin reactions, but that is not the case. Furthermore, adrenalin only gives a short burst of energy, and over time will sap your strength.

> Adrenalin and sympathetic stimulation do not improve muscular performance. Rather they reduce efficiency by increasing lactic acid formation and by interfering with glucose and oxygen utilization. Sudden fear may bring a sudden urge to flee and so provide a powerful spur to action. When this urge leads to successful escape and the danger is past, the effects of sympathetic stimulation quickly subside. But when escape is impossible and fear becomes chronic, the physical and psychological effects of fear soon incapacitate a man for serious work. Mental work becomes impossible because attention is centered on the threatening danger. The central effect of fear...makes it difficult to remember, imagine, or decide on action.[2]

So, in an emergency situation, a person responding with fear – an epinephrin (adrenalin) reaction – will have energy briefly and afterward will feel increasingly weak. The feeling of continuing strength comes from the hormone norepinephrin (noradrenalin) which is associated with the energizing response of anger.

> ...noradranaline, like adrenaline, induces the release of glucose from the liver; but unlike adrenaline, it leaves muscle glycogen untouched. This would mean that noradrenaline secretion increases the blood sugar available to the muscles without breaking down muscle glycogen, and so promotes muscular strength. This would explain why anger gives us the

feeling of being stronger than usual, in contrast to fear which makes us feel weak.[3]

The word "stage-fright" is an unfortunate label because it implies several things which are just not true. Like camera-fright or mike-fright, it suggests that the sensations are caused by an object or place. Actually, the feelings are caused by a change in *relationship* between you and other people. A mike is "feared" only in the sense that when you speak into it your relationship with your listeners is changed and different relationships require different communication skills.

Public speaking provokes an emotional state because when you stand before an audience your communication relationship with those people is different. Perceptions are different, expectations are different, roles are different, and all that is new to you.

The word stage-fright implies also, that there is threat or danger in the situation. Even other labels which have been substituted for stagefright like *speech anxiety* or *communication apprehension* are still synonyms for fear. Anxiety is the label for a fear when the cause is very general in nature or not well defined. The idea that communication is an apprehensive situation similar to phobias – like fear of a snake, or a spider, or heights – is counter-productive because it suggests a possible danger exists.

Terms like anxiety or apprehension are not an improvement over fight-flight theory because they are not related to a specific physiological theory with explanatory power. The inadequacy of the communication anxiety construct has not gone unnoticed.

> The construct integrity of CA (communication anxiety) is threatened for three reasons. First, an alternative construct, generalized anxiety, was nearly as successful in predicting.... Second, the broader conceptual base purported to be tapped by CA was not confirmed. ... Third, the construct integrity of CA is threatened by conceptual obscurity.[4]

The reason why this myth must be dispelled is that if you believe that public speaking is a fearful experience you may attempt coping strategies that are not effective. The most common mistakes are beliefs that you should: just relax, just pretend, or just accept the symptoms. Many speakers believe that those are valid coping techniques. However, those strategies lead to the "sloppy" speech, the "phony" speech, and the "painful" speech.

Mistake 1. just relax. This belief could be stated: if you are an effective speaker in everyday conversation, but in a fearful situation cannot speak well, then you need to get rid of the fear in order to speak effectively.

Some beginning speakers mistakenly think that a person who looks at ease while speaking, really is at ease, and therefore they try to achieve that same appearance by trying to be at ease. The result is usually that they will look like they don't care: they slouch and have no enthusiasm in their delivery. Appearance is often very different from reality, particularly at a distance.

Thinking that if you just get comfortable in front of an audience you'll naturally do the right thing is a big mistake. The truth is that your natural conversational gestures and voice patterns would be ineffective. The gestures would be too small to be seen and they would probably be repetitious and boring. The voice would not be loud enough to be heard and would lack necessary variety, and thus also be boring. Public speaking requires more effort than normal to reach listeners.

But what about people who have the "gift of gab" and can talk off the "top of their head?" Unfortunately, just talking off the top of your head usually sounds exactly like that – sloppy, with no organization, no effective variety or emphasis, no support for ideas, and the ideas are usually common, without adequate development.

Mistake 2. just pretend. Some people think that they can just pretend that they are confident and use different tricks to make it easier to face the audience. The common ones are: "Don't look at their faces, look just above their heads," "Imagine that they are naked, that'll make you feel you have an advantage," "Use a sensational attention-getter to begin the speech and that'll hook them," "Act like you are confident and soon you will be." Well, you may get through a few speeches with those approaches, but you run the risk of continuing to use them until they become habits, very bad habits.

Not making real eye-contact with the audience makes you appear to have a glazed or vacant look. Creating an unreal perception of the audience interferes with establishing real communication with them. Using gimmicks to get attention often results in the attention being on the gimmick – not on your message. If you adopt an artificial role every time you speak your real personality won't be seen and you may appear to be arrogant or insensitive or something other than yourself. Audiences are quite good at seeing through tricks, and consider them the mark of a phony.

You are not adapting to your audience. Using artificial perceptions, role-playing, or "sure-fire" techniques are really defensive, avoidance behaviors which prevent you from learning new speaking skills and also prevent authentic communication with the audience.

Mistake 3. just accept. This is an instance of believing that the degree of your symptoms is related to the degree of your success – the more nervousness, the better you'll do. Some speakers who have excellent speaking skills continue to experience severe symptoms to the point of great discomfort. They are well prepared, have spoken many times, have always done well, and expect to do well again, yet they experience emotional upset way out of line with their previous successes and predictions of future success. Is that desirable or even necessary? No! There are at least two reasons that could account for this inconsistency between their perception of emotional distress and their ability to speak well.

First, some people think they are in a more highly aroused state than they really are.

> Some individuals, for example, will report intense distress and display rapid avoidance when confronted with feared situations, but no evidence of increases in physiological arousal can be detected. Others may show such autonomic increases but differ in the degree to which they are aware of the arousal, the degree of avoidance behavior, the level of reported discomfort, etc.[5]

This was confirmed by another researcher who found that about half of the people who said they had severe anxiety when giving a five minute impromptu speech actually had very low physiological arousal as measured by blood pressure.

> There appear to be two patterns of response that account for over 80% of the sample (N=52) in the present study. One group was characterized by negative cognitions as well as high levels of physiological reactivity. The second group was characterized by identical levels of negative cognitions, but showed a low level of physiological reactivity. ... Almost equal numbers of socially anxious individuals manifested low levels of physiologically reactivity as those demonstrating much higher

responses during the social performance task.[6]

Some people want the severe sensations because in the past they did well when they had those feelings. In spite of the discomfort, they are more afraid of not having them.

Second, *believing fear must be present for you to be effective is just as erroneous as the belief that reducing fear will make you more effective.*

These misunderstandings illustrate ineffective adaptation by people who have learned bad habits instead of new skills. But you can avoid those mistakes and make an effective adaptation. The alternative to the stage-fright model is the model of "stress."

Speech stress. Stress is intensely private and individualized. Suppose you asked some speakers, "How do you feel when you give a speech?" You would probably get two types of answers. "My stomach feels like it's tied in a knot," and "My heart's beating like a triphammer." But if there are two different reactions, what advice would you give? The suggestion that helps one speaker might not help another speaker.

Opposite reactions. In a Clevinger and King[7] study of stage-fright reactions were observed that were exactly opposite to each other. It was noted that some speakers find blood rushes to their face, while for others the blood drains out of their face. Some speakers freeze up becoming immobile, while others fidget with many nervous movements. And some speakers get a dry throat, while others find that saliva accumulates in their mouth.

A similar finding was reported by Borkovec who tested 300 female and 281 male college students with the *Autonomic Perception Questionnaire* to discover individual differences. He found that there were three types of physiological response by the women and two types of response by the men.

> Type I females were found to be associated with high awareness of stomach activity and perspiration when anxious. Type II females were characterized by high awareness of heart activity and muscle tension.... Awareness of heart and stomach activity was characteristic of type III females. Type I males were characterized solely by high awareness of heart activity. ... Stomach activity, perspiration, and frequency of noticing bodily reactions when anxious were characteristic of type II males....[8]

It appears, therefore, that some individuals under stress notice a stronger reaction in the area of their stomach and other people notice greater change in their heart activity, a possible third group has a mixture of both. Different people have different, even opposite, reactions to public speaking and that does not fit the "stage-fright" model.

Speech stress is a label which relates public speaking to a large body of research and a powerful theory which describes the necessary preparation of the body for learning new skills.

The response continuum. An audience situation is an unique communication setting requiring highly developed communication skills, but it is not an emergency reaction, and neither is it like the prolonged stress that leads to "burnout" or psychosomatic problems. There is a continuum of defense responses made by the body to different degrees of stress.

> In seeking any understanding of the so-called diseases of stress, it is important to study three phases or aspects of stress reactions: the acute emergency reaction (Cannon's fight-flight reaction); the ability to handle stress as time passes; and the sustained or chronic stress reaction.[9]

Different bodily processes are triggered in response to changes in our environment and they vary depending on immediacy and duration. First, the body is protected by a *reflex* action which is very fast and very brief. Second, the organism is protected by the *fight-flight* response which permits a strong emergency response. Third, the body has a *stress* response (general adaptation syndrome) for continuing situations of longer duration which helps you adapt to the new situation. In the long term, you either adapt or you will experience severe physical or emotional problems.

CONTINUUM OF BEHAVIORAL RESPONSES

Immediate	Emergency	Short term	Long range
Reflex action	Fight-flight	Stress coping	New skill or Burnout

When you place public speaking on that continuum, you can see that only an impromptu speech could possibly fall in the emergency category, but prepared speeches call for a short term adaptation, and those experiences may lead to the development of new skills in the long term.

The stress model of emotional response includes both situations where the pressures on a person are negative (distress), or in a case like public speaking, where the pressure is positive (eustress). For example, a promotion in your job causes stress because advancement means you have to function at a higher level of effectiveness, accept new responsibilities, and meet greater expectations.

An athletic team that is undefeated carries increased pressure into every new game it plays. Getting married is a happy occasion, but there is great stress on the couple who anticipate a future with increased obligations. And that's the type of pressure in public speaking, you are adjusting to a higher level of performance in a new situation which is stressful, but also very desirable. Public speaking is an eustressful experience; stress caused by higher expectations.

> Adaptability is probably the most distinctive characteristic of life. ...indeed there is perhaps even a certain parallelism between the degree of aliveness and the extent of adaptability in every animal – in every man.[10]
>
> ...stress is the common denominator of all adaptive reactions in the body.[11]

When the human body experiences stress from any source (physical, mental, biological, chemical, etc.) it makes a generalized response which consists of three stages. In the first stage there is an alarm reaction caused by the stressor. In the second stage the body responds with hormone secretions which make resistance possible. In the third stage the body achieves adaptation, or if not successful, the defenses of the body become exhausted.

The most important thing to remember is that in stage two the body scretes hormones which are antagonistic to each other.

> ...one of the most characteristic features of the G.A.S. (general adaptation syndrome) is that its various defensive mechanisms are always based on combinations of these two types of response: advance and retreat. It is essentially an antagonistic response, that is, one designed to activate two opposing forces.[12]

For example, when you are coping with stress your body secretes both adrenalin and noradrenalin. Adrenalin is associated with a "fear" response and noradrenalin is associated with an "anger" response, but together they allow the body to find the appropriate balance between energized action and inhibition of action which best suits the situation.

The relationship between adrenalin and noradrenalin is complex. At low levels they produce the same effects, and each one may trigger the release of the other, adrenalin can even be converted into noradrenalin. While at low levels it doesn't make much difference since most people can handle a moderate level of arousal, but at higher levels the effects of the two hormones diverge and then coping is a critical concern and different coping techniques are needed for different individuals.

Balanced response. If we apply this theory to public speaking it would be something like this: The speaking situation can be a stressful occurrence because of prior experience, expectation of audience demands, awareness of personal inadequacies and/or many other factors. Thus, 1) the speaker must adapt to a new situation (alarm stage), 2) the body produces an increase in opposite-acting hormones (resistance stage), and 3) the speaker finds the best balance of energy utilization for that situation. Until there is balanced adaptation there may be some extreme reactions, like freezing-up or random fidgeting. Only adrenalin and noradrenalin were discussed, but in the internal balancing act many other hormonal and neural transmitter changes follow the same principle.

We might compare it to the thrills that people seek at a theme park. On those exciting rides the emotions run high, hormones are secreted, and our body responds to the new experience. But we know that we are not in danger and while our body is under stress we may interpret that as fun.

Personality and situations. There has also been some debate whether communication apprehension is a personality trait of the individual or a state caused by the situation.[13] Funkenstein researched how college students reacted to both emergency and continuing stresses. But their initial response did not determine whether they would be successful in adapting to persistent stress.

> There was no relation between the emotion reported during the acute emergency reaction and whether or not a man was able to master stress.[14]

In fact, he isolated two different aspects of an individual's personality. Not only do we have a personal style of stress response, but we have a personal style of adaptation.

> Personality factors which measured the deeper aspects of personality – such as the perception of family constellations, the internal concept of self, and the fantasies of the men about aggression and its consequences – correlated with acute emergency reactions; those personality measures which were more related to function – such as the interpersonal measures, the ability to assess reality, and the integration of the personality – correlated with the ability to handle stress on a time continuum.
>
> These results suggested that the acute emergency reactions and its personality correlates represented one aspect of personality, the basic disposition, whereas the ability to handle stress as time passed represented another aspect of personality, namely, ego function.[15]

While a *predisposition* to act in an emergency is related to personality patterns set early in life, the *behavior* in a stressful communication situation calls on all your experience and skills developed up to the present moment in time. Your tendency to immediately respond with anger or fear when under stress is probably developed when you you were young (different people respond differently).

However, your ability to cope with a stressful situation over the long run changes with new communication experiences (you learn by doing).

> Zenker finds that most people's public communication problems, parallel their private communication problems, although they come into his classes denying it. "I've had people swear to me that they are dynamic and forceful in one-to-one situations but turn into shy, retiring creatures in front of large groups. The truth of the matter is that they are shy and retiring creatures in both situations. The way people communicate represents the sum total of the personality they've developed up to the point when they walk into my class."[16]

This understanding leads to a powerful conclusion. If it is true that all your other communication experiences contribute to your public speaking skills the relationship will be reciprocal. That is, if you learn to adapt to stress in the public speaking situation you will have increased confidence in other communication settings. So those stresses that you have in other social situations can be reduced because you have faced the public speaking challenge.

In summary, the sensations you feel that are associated with public speaking are caused by an anticipated or perceived change in your communication relationship. It is not a fear response, but a preparation for new skill learning. It consists of tension between opposite functions within the body which make possible flexibility and control both in communicating and in learning new skills. Those two forces will not be exactly equal, so that's why some people will have different, even opposite, symptoms. And since individuals experience different sensations each person must find the adaptation (coping) strategies which are most effective for them. However, ultimately the only real solution for everyone is to learn the new skills appropriate for the situation.

Individual differences. One speaker's confidence may rest more in content, organization and language skills. Another speaker's confidence may be based more on creativity and delivery skills.

Some may have more symptoms of stress in the upper respiratory region, shortness of breath and racing heart, while others may have more symptoms in the region of the stomach.

Some people find it helpful to rehearse in front of a mirror so they can see their posture and gestures. But others find the mirror too distracting. So don't use a mirror if it interferes with your concentration.

Some will find it helpful if a friend listens and evaluates the speech. But other people need to practice alone.

No simple formula or easy explanation would account for the different insecurities of all the many personalities that appear at a speaker's podium. But fortunately, you can attack the problem on three levels of functioning: mental, emotional and physical.

> Cognitive behavior, motor behavior, and physiological reactions may be separately influenced by different environmental conditions at different points in time and may even obey different learning principles. Yet because of their potential interaction, changes in one response component due to the direct manipulation of its conditions may ultimately affect subsequent changes in the response of one or both of the remaining components.[17]

Mental preparation. It is a great help to know when you are prepared to speak. Using the *readiness inentory* form, review all the work you have done and estimate how well you think you have done it. If you don't think you have prepared well enough then you should go back and rework those areas that are weak. If you score considerably more pluses than minuses, then you are probably as ready as you'll ever be.

Emotional preparation. Excuses are negative programming. We know that one defense mechanism is to tell others how poorly we'll do in order to lower their expectations of our performance. Then it is easier for us to meet those expectations.

But others are suspicious when you make those apologies and if you do well you may lose credibility. But that's not the greatest harm you are inflicting on yourself.

Self-fulfilling prophecy. That's the tendency to conform to our statements about ourselves – whether they are true or false, positive or negative. If you make enough excuses, that alone could make you fail. If people ask how you are going to do, you can honestly say, "I'm going to try my best." You can admit to nervousness without exaggerating. Don't be negative.

Projection. Another process is called projection which is the tendency to ascribe to others, thoughts or feelings that you have. In this context you may project on your audience the same attitudes that you have when you are a member of an audience.

For example, when you listen to speakers are you critical? Do you look for mistakes? Do you tend to disagree with their ideas? If that is the case, then when you give a speech you will probably think the audience is looking for your faults. You remember all the mistakes you have criticized in others and will be afraid that you will make those same mistakes.

If, on the contrary, when you are in an audience you appreciate the efforts of the speaker, look for what you can gain from the speech, and notice the good qualities, then you could feel very differently when it is your turn to speak. It would be natural for you to feel that the audience is supportive.

I'm not saying, "Do unto others as you would have them do unto you," but rather, "You do to yourself (in your own mind) what you have done to others." A positive attitude toward others who speak, and toward yourself as a speaker, go together.

Offense versus defense. Some speakers gain a feeling of confidence by emphasizing a strong offense, others by capitalizing on a strong defense. An offensive stance would emphasize your personal motivation with attitudes like:

I can learn from mistakes that I might make.

My message is more important than my ability to perform.

I only have to give it my best effort.

Even if I don't meet all their expectations I can live with that.

I have some information that they need.

I have more strengths than deficiencies.

A defensive stance would consist of attitudes that emphasize the audience's interest:

They wouldn't have asked me to speak if they didn't have confidence in me.

They will not be able to see the nervousness that I feel inside.

They will empathize with my situation.

They will appreciate the time and energy I have put into my preparation.

They don't want to be bored so they will be looking for good ideas.

They don't want their time wasted so they want me to do well.

Even if you are speaking on a controversial issue to an audience who holds opposite attitudes to your own, the situation still has positive elements. Audiences want you to present your ideas clearly. It is in their best interest for you to communicate well your thoughts.

Self-talk. By carefully planned self-instruction a person may achieve indirect control over stress responses: l) monitor your symptoms, 2) place a positive interpretation on the sensations, and 3) reinforce any success with positive statements.

> The first step in the change process is the client's becoming an observer of his own behavior. Through heightened awareness and deliberate attention, the client monitors, with increased sensitivity, his thoughts, feelings, and/or interpersonal behaviors. If the client's behavior is to change, then what he now says to himself, and/or imagines, must initiate a new behavioral chain, one which is incompatible with his maladaptive behaviors. The third step in the change process, what the client says to himself about his newly acquired behaviors, determines whether the behavioral change will be maintained

and will generalize.[18]

You need to analyze very precisely what symptoms, feelings, or tensions you experience. Then you need to decide what those sensations mean to you, do they signal trouble or do they mean you are prepared to do well? Picture yourself speaking more effectively because of those feelings. At the conclusion of your speech you should recall the positive qualities of your delivery.

Self-regulation procedures.

Stage l. Objective observation (when you feel stress).

How do my legs feel? any tremor? any tension?

Are there any sensations in my solar-plexus?

How do my arms and hands feel? tremor? tension?

What's my breathing like? any shortness of breath?

Is there any difference in my heart rate?

Are my lips or mouth moist or dry?

Is my body temperature any different from normal?

Are my symptoms mild? average? severe?

Stage 2. Positive Interpretation (mental self-talk).

The tension I feel in my legs, arms or other muscles of my body is available energy so that I may move easily while in front of my audience.

I need more energy because my gestures need to be somewhat larger than the gestures I use in a private conversation.

The energy I feel allows me to speak so that I can be heard by everyone. I need that energy because I need to project my voice.

My increased arousal makes me more alert. I can observe more accurately the responses of individuals in the audience.

My audience is very relaxed and I need vitality and enthusiasm to hold their interest and stimulate their thoughts.

It is naturally thrilling to express my thoughts to many other people at one time.

Stage 3. Positive Evaluation (after the speech is over).

When did my speech stress symptoms start to decrease?

What things went well?

Physical preparation. A researcher named Paul[19] at a large midwestern university selected the most anxious 96 speakers from 710 students enrolled in public speaking classes. They were divided into four groups.

One group received no special help of any kind outside of their class and by the end of the semester 17% of them had eliminated their fear of speaking. They benefited from giving speeches in class and were able to learn by themselves how to adapt to audiences.

Another group were in a placebo condition; that is, they were led to believe that they were being helped, but got no real advice or coping techniques. Just being singled out for attention seemed to encourage them because 47% showed significant reduction in their fear. A supportive climate is a powerful aid to the fearful speaker.

A third group were given intensive psychotherapy designed to help them get insight into what caused their fears. Understanding of themselves helped 47% of that group, also. However, insight into childhood trauma or similar fears was not any more useful than simple encouragement.

The fourth group was trained in desensitization and 100% of that group had a significant reduction in their fear response when speaking. Other research has confirmed the effectiveness of desensitization.[20] The technique is not difficult to use, but it takes a lot of practice before results will be evident.

As described in chapter eight, the first thing to master is the art of relaxation and then you must maintain that relaxed state while you picture yourself in different situations that progressively approach and culminate in the imaginary delivery of your speech before your audience.

Variation. It is also possible to modify this technique. For example, instead of sitting in a chair you might lie down instead. You might also modify the procedures as follows:

After attaining a relaxed state focus on your muscles. (10 seconds)

Visualize an audience which is receptive and enjoying your speech. (10 seconds)

Relax and focus on your muscles. (10 seconds)

Visualize a bored audience and see yourself pep up your delivery. (10 seconds)

Relax and focus on your muscles. (10 seconds)

Visualize an unreceptive audience and see yourself winning them over. (10 seconds)

Relax and focus on your muscles. (10 seconds)

Repeat sequence.

etc.

These techniques may be repeated often, daily is best, until it is time to give your speech. Public speaking can be exhilarating if you have trust in your preparation, and in your audience, and in yourself. Facing a challenge is a fundamentally healthy human experience.

Part III, Chapter 18

Speaking

Personal effectiveness decisions. You may be surprised to learn that about a third of the speakers tested did not review their speech just prior to speaking, because that increased their stress.

About twice as many speakers use visualization compared to positive self-talk to cope with stress. Only a few use muscle-tensing as a relaxation technique.

Not many speakers perceive their delivery as low-energy, though my observation would differ from this. Their feelings of speech stress probably inflate their evaluation of movement and voice.

About half the speakers do not try to change their delivery according to their speech purpose.

About half the speakers have little awareness of the audience while speaking.

About half the speakers do not try to adapt to audience feedback. This figure also reflects their personal perception, not the perception of myself or the audience.

One third give shorter speeches than planned, one third run over, and one third don't deviate much from their plan.

In summary, some speakers derive security primarily from their material. They gather content, they organize it well, they may write it out completely, and they usually rehearse it several times.

Others rely more on delivery. They are confident even though the ideas and words are only loosely structured in general terms, because they feel that a spontaneous delivery is more important. Their ability to make it all come together in the presentation is their strength and the looser organization allows for flexibility. So while both types of speakers rehearse until they "know the speech," one person's idea of "knowing" is not the same as another's, one is more specific and the other is more general.

Therefore, to improve your speaking, ask someone who: 1) has done a lot of speaking, 2) is familiar with different speaking styles, and 3) knows the reason behind different speaking styles. A professional approach to speaking means that you are continually seeking the best information available and continually working to improve your speaking.

Myth of passive delivery. This myth is that a speaker should not move or gesture. That would be throwing away the power of the platform. Movement, gesture, and voice is the advantage that the writer does not have – why would you not use these powerful tools to convey your message? Granted, if you had a message of dire consequence – "Your child has been kidnapped," "There's a flood coming" – no one would care about your delivery. However, how often do you deliver that kind of message? For almost every speech that you will ever give, delivery will be critical to your success.

Our nervous system is designed to detect change in the environment and then to match that change to memory and to goals. If it has relevance to the individual, then attention will focus on that data until the degree of relevance declines or another change is noticed.

> If he (the speaker) is new to the audience, or if the occasion itself is novel he can expect the majority of listeners to focus their eyes upon him. When the newness wears off, if the scenery remains static, if the visual field is not changed, the restless nervous systems of members of the audience will compel their eyes to stray elsewhere. The eyes may return occasionally, infrequently, or not at all, unless the speaker has planned to change the scenery by providing some form of movement.[1]
>
> The human body was built to move. ... There is no single, perfect posture that one can assume for the duration of a speech. Even if there were, the body becomes stiff when held too long in one position, and the audience would be visibly bored without changes of visual stimulation.[2]
>
> ...he (the effective speaker) regains attention with a frequency approaching the audiences maximum speed of attention shift. ... The effective speaker not only plans to regain attention, he deliberately plans to release his audience from attention to the speech at strategic points. The idea here is sim-

ply that full, constant attention is functionally impossible for the human nervous system.[3]

The alternative to the myth of passive delivery is audience adaptation.

Coping. Your pre-delivery coping is a last minute repetition of your stress-lowering rehearsals. You reject negative thoughts and decide on the basis of your preparation that you are indeed ready to speak. Then you build emotional strength by analyzing honestly your physical symptoms and engaging in self-talk which is positive.

A long yawn (8 to 10 seconds) stretches the muscles around your mouth and throat and thus will relax them. A shrill voice, a weak voice, a breathy voice, or a raspy voice, can be largely due to the tension in muscles attached to your vocal folds. When they are relaxed your voice tends to be stronger and more resonant.

Tense your major muscle groups and then allow them to relax deeply. Picture yourself speaking confidently.

If your heart is beating fast, you need an increased amount of oxygen. However if you take deep breaths too quickly you may hyperventilate. So while inhaling, count silently to six, then on your exhalation also count to six. On your next breath count to seven while breathing in, and count to seven while breathing out. Then on your next breath make it an eight count on both inhalation and exhalation, etc. The mental counting insures that each breath gets progressively slower.

Remember when you walk up and stand at the lectern that you can pause a second before starting to speak. And then, you can capitalize on the "energy" that you have available which will make you more effective.

Audience adaptation. The process of communication is most clearly seen when listeners are least constrained. For example, suppose that you were standing on a soap box in Hyde Park, England and were trying to attract an audience. That park is famous for the many speakers who expound on various social, political, religious and philosophical ideas. Your first attempts to draw a crowd would almost certainly be failures.

But if you were motivated by a message that you thought was very important, and persisted with daily repetition, over a relatively short period of time you would learn how to attract and hold the interest of an audience.

That type of experience has occurred to people in many different situations. People learn extremely well in situations that are realistic, interactive, and intrinsically rewarding.

Take another example, comedians learn how to "work" an audience from direct interaction with them. Consider a master of ceremonies' job which is to change a crowd into an audience, and they do it every night! Those individuals are professionals – they know their craft. And it is exactly what every public speaker needs to know.

A Hyde Park speaker learns fast because the feedback is clear. If you are saying something interesting a crowd gathers, if you are saying something uninteresting or don't keep the interest, the people walk away. You soon learn that when people are stopping you had better continue to develop the ideas that attracted them. If people start to leave, you had better change from what you are saying to find other ideas which will hold them. As you gain more experience you learn what kinds of things the people in your audience want to hear about and what things they are not interested in.

Now look at a comedian or master of ceremonies. He has a prepared sequence of jokes. When the audience is responding positively he continues with his planned routine, but if he gets a negative response he deviates from his plan and quickly does or says something else which is guaranteed to get a laugh. That "something else" is a repertory of material which he has used in the past and knows will work. So if a joke falls flat, he quickly turns to an old joke or comment that will be sure to provoke a laugh. "Hello, are you still there?" "It's all right to laugh now!" "This audience is fired!" "That's no way to treat a veteran!" etc. He gets them responding and speeds up the tempo so the response comes faster. That briefly, is what happens when an entertainer is "working" an audience.

Observe the behaviors occuring in an audience. Essentially, feedback can be generalized into three categories: positive, negative, or mixed. The mixed response is regarded as negative because you can only deal effectively with a positive or a negative reaction. You need to remember only two principles:

1) receiving positive response – continue,
2) receiving negative response – change.

Therefore, a professional:

1) Has a prepared content and delivery plan,
2) Has a repertory of content material and delivery techniques,
3) Monitors the audience for positive and negative feedback,
4) Adapts the message when necessary.

Your content repertory consists largely of material left over from preparing your speech. Your delivery repertory consists of movement and gestures you have practiced in rehearsal and used in previous speeches.

Audience adaptation is built on a foundation of thoughtful consideration of your speaker-audience relationship. Good preparation gives you back-up options that you can use in response to audience feedback. That reservoir of information increases your self-confidence. Adapt-ability can be planned. Ability-to-adapt can be learned.

Requisite variety. An understanding of the dynamics of speaking requires understanding Ashby's law of requisite variety.[4]

> There is now ample evidence...that when an organism perceives he is forming an image, an internal representation of his environment. ...when an organism acts he is making an external representation of his plans, the neural programs in his head – his motives, intentions, and values.[5]

That is why this book has stressed the importance of your self-image, your audience-image and idea-image relationships in organization.

The law can be stated, "The capacity of an organism to regulate, to control, can at best equal its capacity to process information."[6] It describes the relationship between perception and action and therefore defines effectiveness.

Your repertory consists of all your knowledge, attitudes, and skills. Constraints are the challenges in the situation. If you have relevant knowledge and sufficient skill in your repertory which matches or exceeds the requirements of a particular situation you are able to act confidently, expending only the energy necessary to do the job.

If, on the other hand, the demands of the situation exceed your ability to respond appropriately, you are unable to act, and therefore become emotional.

> When the variety of perceptions exceeds to some consider-

> able extent the repertory of action available to the organism he is motivated to ... extend his repertory. Whenever this attempt fails, is non-reinforced, frustrated, or interrupted, the organism becomes of necessity emotional, i.e., he must resort to mechanisms of self-regulation, self-control.
>
> ...emotion expresses the relationship between perception and action. Another way of stating this is to say that emotion relates information processing and control mechanisms, image, and plan. ...whenever the organism is operating beyond the bounds of requisite variety he becomes motivated, emotional, or both.
>
> ...the expression of emotions indicates that an internal process of control, rather than action, is operative in the organism's attempt to accomplish requisite variety. ...they suggest, however, that action at the moment, for one reason or another, is infeasible.[7]

If you cannot act, you pause to figure out what to do next. During that pause, you may feel frustrated, confused, fearful, angry, etc. You are motivated to learn new skills, but while you are trying to create a new behavioral response, you have to control yourself, you hold back actions or decisions that you know would not be effective. Emotion is arousal associated with restructuring of habits, devising new actions, "freezing," random action, inappropriate, or excessive action.

> Motivation and emotion thus go hand in hand. But motive implies action, the formation of an external representation; e-motion, on the other hand, implies the opposite, i.e., to be out of, or away from action.
>
> ... Motivation and emotion, action and passion, to be effective and to be affective: these are the organism's polar mechanisms for accomplishing requisite variety when he perceives more than he can accomplish.[8]

This matching of repertory to speaking constraints is the primary perception which triggers speech stress. The bodily response which results when the repertory is insufficient is the general adaptation syndrome which was described in the previous section on lowering stress. Out task then, is to *build a repertory of concepts, and skills that are equal to, or surpass the demands of a speaking situation.* A text on leadership says,

> For leadership to be effective, then, it must be as complex as the information environment of which it is a part. ...

> Leadership, then, is effective to the degree that it can adapt its messages to the constraints of a situation. Leaders skilled in competent communication are able to adapt or modify their messages to meet the needs of particular situations. Leadership communication may need to be simple, clear, and direct in some situations but complex, ambiguous, and subtle in others. Effective leaders possess a large repertoire of communication skills that they draw from to adapt their messages to a variety of situations.[9]

Maintaining lead time. Delivery problems attributed to stress are primarily the result of an overload of demands. That is, any one task if taken singly could be handled, but when there are too many you can't manage them all at once. It's like trying to juggle. Suppose you know how to juggle three balls in the air. There isn't any additional knowledge needed to keep four or five balls in the air, but it's much harder to do. Even if you know how to juggle, it will take practice to develop your coordination to that new level of proficiency.

So also with speaking; you know what ideas are interesting, you know a good story when you hear one, you know how to speak expressively, you know how to gesture, etc., but you've never put it all together when standing in front of an audience. Coordinating the entire effort will take time and practice.

The mark of skilled behavior is "lead time" or the anticipation of the next movement well in advance so that there is a smooth flow from the completion of one action to the beginning of the next action. Skill means that decision making is operating well ahead of action taking. There is no break in the flow; there is no more energy expended than is necessary. This continues so long as the repertory matches the requirements of the situation.

Any activity that involves multiple skills is accomplished by mastering each skill to the point where only minimal awareness is necessary for its execution.

If your content is mastered to the point where you are sure of your memory, then your attention can be directed to your delivery.

Standing comfortably without slouching or having an awkward posture is not a behavior that should require your attention, it should be natural. The same is true of speaking with variety in your voice and gesturing naturally with your hands. Speaking with a loud enough voice to be heard must be a behavior which is mastered to the level of habit.

When you need only part of your attention on language choices then you can pay more attention to the audience response. At this point you have sufficient awareness available to adapt to that audience response and modify your delivery, language, or content, if necessary.

So the value of a repertory of information and speaking skills is that it helps you keep your lead time. Driving a car, flying a plane, and public speaking have in common the necessity of being able to monitor several things going on at the same time, anticipating things that could happen, and making appropriate responses if the unexpected occurs. Freezing at the controls or at the speaker's stand occurs when the demands of the situation exceed the repertory of plans and skills required to cope with that situation. The task of managing all those skills, shifting the appropriate amount of awareness to different behavior at the necessary moment is a complex task, but can be learned with practice.

Audience involvement. Sometimes in order to heighten audience interest you ask individuals for their input so that they will then feel a greater commitment to listen. There are three ways of involving an audience directly. One is answering questions after the speech is over, the second is inviting questions before you speak and the third is taking questions during your speech. They all follow the same principles.

Questions after. This is relatively easy to do. 1) Keep your answers short – don't make another speech. 2) If you don't know the answer, say so. You don't have to have an answer for everything. 3) If you get a question requiring a long explanation – say so, and invite the person to stay and talk with you later. 4) If you get an hostile question, be polite. 5) When a significant pause occurs, end the questioning period by thanking the audience.

Questions before. You begin by announcing your subject and asking the audience what questions they have about that topic. As each question is asked you repeat the question, sometimes rewording it to conform more closely to one of the main points in your speech. You might write the questions on a chalkboard or paper pad and when enough questions have been asked to cover your main points you bring the questioning to an end.

You announce in what order you will answer the questions (which is the order of your speech) and proceed with your talk. If you have prepared well you will have the basic answers to the general questions that people will ask. If you should get a specific question for which you are unprepared you simply say that you can't answer that question at this time.

Questions during. With this approach you begin your speech by discussing the first main point in your speech (which you anticipate will provoke high interest) and then ask if there is a question. Again, you'll usually get a question about another aspect of your subject on which you are prepared.

Take the question, relate it to one of the other main points in your prepared speech and explain that idea in full. Then ask for another question. You continue until you have covered all the main points that you had prepared and then thank the audience for their questions.

What happens is that you work in all the ideas you wanted to discuss, but you let the audience determine the order in which they hear the ideas. Naturally, you would use these approaches in an informal setting and only after you feel quite expert on the subject matter.

They illustrate that *your adaptation to an audience can be no better than your preparation.*

Speaking. The challenging situation that a speaker faces is competing with every other stimulus in the environment and meeting every listener's hidden agenda. You must be the most interesting presence in the situation. To accomplish that, you must make three general modifications to your usual mode of communicating.

First, your movements need to be larger so they can be seen at a distance. Second, your voice needs to be louder so it can be heard at a distance. That is not difficult – it is mainly being aware of the need to do it. For example, when you are outdoors and call to someone at a distance your voice and gesture automatically increase in volume and size. "Hey, come here a minute!"

You should be aware that microphones have generally reduced the effectiveness of speakers. People assume they only need to talk to the mike and their voice will hold the attention of the audience. However, focusing on the mike results in a flat voice, the expressiveness is gone, the energy is lacking, it is uninteresting. People who use a mike effectively speak past it, not to it, and project to a larger audience.

The third modification is to maintain interest for a longer time than a typical conversation. You know that if you are telling a long story to someone, sometimes you have to emphasize parts of the story to keep his or her attention. The same thing is true in public speaking. There must be variety to keep interest for a longer period of time.

Posture – the foundation. Without good posture there will be no physical movement. When you lean on the lectern or stand with your weight on one leg you can't move. Standing with your weight equally balanced on both legs makes it easy to move.

Movement mastery. Trying to prevent movement when you are physically "charged up" will result in mannerisms. You can eliminate random actions by moving and gesturing.

Eye contact – the precursor. If you don't look at the audience you won't have gestures. Typically, eye-contact with the audience leads to making some gestures. You are figuratively reaching out to communicate, first with your eyes, then with your hands.

Gesture mastery. It is helpful to know the natural order in a child's development of gestural control. Control of movement is *cephal* to *caudal,* that is, control of the head precedes control of lower limbs. Control of movement is also *proximo* to *distal;* it begins at the centerline of the body and moves toward the extremities. Learning effective movement and gesture in public speaking will follow that same order. You'll find it easier to show more facial expression before you will be comfortable taking a few steps. You'll also be more comfortable making small gestures close to your body before you extend your arms to make larger gestures.

Establish a flexible relationship between your hands and the lectern. Your hands should not grasp for support, hide from view, or remain constantly in one place. In other words, change the position of your hands in reference to the lectern. You may place both hands on the lectern, or take your hands off the lectern, you may hold the sides of the lectern, you may place one hand on the lectern, etc.

Begin with small hand gestures. Get your hands up in front of you, get them up off the lectern and they will move naturally.

Establish a flexible relationship between your feet and the lectern. Your feet need not be anchored to one spot nor should there be any random movement. You can take a step or two to one side or to the other, you can take a step backward if you choose. You can even move in front of the lectern if you want. The lectern does not control your position.

Integrate gesture with movement. As emphasis increases it involves the whole body – you gesture and take a step at the same time. Both hands and feet are part of the overall pattern. Of course, the emphasis should be appropriate to the audience size, the subject matter, and your personality.

Voice variety. Mastery of voice also follows a natural order of development. The four aspects of sound are: volume, pitch, rate and quality. And that is also the order of difficulty in gaining control. Changes in quality of the voice, for most people however, are not necessary. That kind of work is usually reserved for a course in voice and diction.

Volume. The easiest thing for a speaker to consciously manipulate is his or her volume or loudness. Speaking louder and then softer can be planned or be a response to audience feedback, but the ability to change the level of loudness should be developed by every speaker.

Pitch. The next easiest task is to pay attention to the inflection of your voice as reflected in a wider range of pitch changes. Some pitch changes occur naturally when you speak louder or softer. Changes will also occur naturally when you place emphasis on particular words.

Rate. Then you work on your rate of speaking, both talking faster and talking slower – being able to do both within the same speech. Changing rate at crucial points is a powerful way to communicate the importance of certain ideas to your audience. That also gives you the ability to pause for emphasis. In fact, one of the marks of the experienced speaker is using a deliberate, dramatic pause. The combination of pitch and rate changes makes an expressive voice.

Periodically, as you give your speech, run through a mental checklist:

Feet – am I standing with sloppy posture? Should I move?

Hands – any distracting movements? Should I gesture?

Voice – Am I speaking loud enough? Do I have variety in my voice? Am I speaking too fast or too slow?

Eyes – Am I looking at all of the audience? Am I looking at faces of individuals?

Language delivery patterns. Relating your delivery to language also has a pattern. Speaking directly to the audience readily provokes gestures, "Raise you hands if any of you...."

The next easiest gestures may be those related to transitional statements, "My second point...," "On the other hand...."

Third, introductory and summary sentences very naturally call for a gesture, "Now the three important ideas are...."

Next easy is emotion-laden words or statements, "Can you believe that?" "It's ridiculous!"

The important thing to remember is that it takes effort for a listener to understand the message of a speech. Delivery makes new ideas easy to understand and remember.

Evaluating. There is no consensus among public speaking teachers on an effective assessment instrument. Not only are various types of evaluation forms found in different textbooks, but some texts don't even offer an instrument. A common practice for teachers is to construct their own evaluation form.

This lack of uniformity is because we really don't have a consensus on some things that we teach. Some teachers insist that a speaker should stand behind a lectern while others teach their students to move away from it. Some teach students to speak from notecards, others teach that a speaker should not use notes at all. Etcetera. It's not difficult to find different advice by different teachers.

Every well known instrument puts more weight on content than delivery. However, according to Mehrabian and Wiener, "Generalizing, we can say that a person's nonverbal behavior has more bearing than his words on communicating feelings or attitudes to others."[10] Therefore, since nonverbal behavior is so powerful in shaping the meaning of the verbal, it should have at least equal weight in assessment.

Speech Progress Chart. Presented at the 1994 Speech Communication Association convention, this assessment instrument consists of speech variables depicted in a graphic format.[11] Each scale is given four common grade divisions: A, B, C, D. This continuum of values is familiar and more meaningful than arbitrary numbers. F is not included because failure is not-giving-a-speech at all. In addition, each position of the scale is labeled with descriptive words.

Casandra Book summarizes research by herself and others by saying, "atomistic, impersonal comments were consistently perceived as most helpful...."[12] In other words, the more specific the description the more helpful the information is considered by the speaker. However, in being more specific, we see that different variables have different patterns of development. The law of requisite variety applies to evaluation. The complexity of an assessment measure, must be equal to the complexity of the behavior being evaluated.

Therefore, each scale conforms to the degree of complexity of the observable speaking behavior. For example, voice volume is a simple variable which ranges on a continuum from weak to strong. But voice rate is more complex because the rate may be either too slow or too fast, the ideal being in the middle between the two extremes. Only a graphic format makes it possible to deal with both simple and complex variables.

The scales for the speaking variables are also spatially arranged to facilitate evaluation. Organizational variables are distributed so the introduction is at the top of the page, followed by a preview, the transition variable is placed in the middle of the form, and the review and conclusion are at the end of the form.

Delivery variables are grouped on one side of the page and content variables on the other side to give equal weight. The delivery variables are arranged in order of decreasing impact so the more dominant are considered first.

Therefore, the rater can start at the top of the chart as the speaker begins, check the variables progressively and the evaluation will be completed when the speech ends.

Another powerful advantage of the graphic type of format is that if a change occurs during the speech (for example, a weak voice becomes stronger) a new mark may be made and an arrow drawn to indicate the direction of the change. So the form makes possible not just an average rating for a speech variable over the entire speech, but a description of significant change on speech variables during the speech.

With the increased precision, non-expert members of an audience should be able to give an evaluation comparable to that of a speech teacher. Wiseman and Barker found, "...when students are provided specific communication criteria they are able to evaluate similarly to instructors...."[13]

To assign a grade, only a few seconds are required to make a summary evaluation of the delivery, another summary for the content, and the two can be averaged. However, the average is not mathematically precise because not all variables are equal. In other words, it is an approximation, though it is an improvement over the traditional simplistic forms.

Endnotes

II:6 ORGANIZING PLANS

1. Gerald M. Goldhaber, "Organizational Communication: State of the Art," *Vital Speeches of the Day,* Feb. 15, 1976.

III:10 A PROFESSIONAL APPROACH

1. Klaus Drippendorff, "The Past of Communication's Hoped-For Future," *Journal of Communication,* 1993, vol. 43, no. 3, p. 18.
2. Gregory J. Sheperd, "Communication as Influence: Definitional Exclusion," *Communication Studies,* 1992, vol. 43, no. 4, p. 216.
3. Margaret J. Wheatley, *Leadership and the New Science,* San Francisco, CA: Barrett-Koehler Pub., 1993, p. 6.
4. Paul Newell Campbell, *Rhetoric and Ritual,* Encino, CA: Dickenson Pub. Co. Inc., 1972, p. 222.
5. Campbell, p. 226.
6. Campbell, p. 227.
7. Thomas P. Whitney, trans., Alecksandr I. Solzhenitsyn, *The Nobel Lecture on Literature,* New York, NY: Harper and Row, 1972, pp. 37-38.
8. NSA's Code of Professional Ethics, Tempe, AZ , National Speakers Association,.
9. Peter M. Senge, *The Fifth Discipline,* New York, NY: Doubleday, 1990, p. 73.

III:11 LIVE SPEAKING SITUATIONS

1. George Mandler, *Mind and Emotion,* pp. 123-124.
2. Leonard Zunn, *Contact: The First Four Minutes,* New York, NY: Ballantine Books, 1972, p. 6.

3. D. A. Norman, "Memory while Shadowing," *Quarterly Journal of Experimental Psychology,* 21, Feb. 1969, pp. 85-93, in Andrew D.Wolvin, Roy M. Berko, Darlyn R. Wolvin, *The Public Speaker/The Public Listener.,* Boston, MA: Houghton Mifflin Co., 1993, p. 25.
4. Blaine Goss, *Processing Communication,* Belmont, CA: Wadsworth Pub. Co., 1982, p. 33.
5. William James, "The Varieties of Attention," *The Principles of Psychology,* New York, NY: Dover Pub., Inc., 1950, p. 421, in Daniel Goleman and Richard J. Davidson, *Consciousness: Brain, States of Awareness, and Mysticism,* New York, NY: Harper & Row, Pub., 1979, p. 44.
6. Robert Ornstein and Paul Ehrlich, *New World, New Mind,* New York, NY: Simon & Schuster, Inc., 1989, p. 4.
7. Daniel J. O'Keefe, *Persuasion: Theory and Research,* Newbury Park, CA: Sage Pub., 1990, p. 132.
8. O'Keefe, p. 133.
9. O'Keefe, pp. 144-145.
10. Campbell, p. 103.
11. Campbell, p. 227.
12. Albert Mehrabian and M. Wiener, "Decoding of Inconsistent Communications," *Journal of Personality and Social Psychology,* 6, 1967, pp. 109-114.
13. D. Coon, "Introduction to Psychology and the Biology of Emotion: A Structural Approach," *American Psychologist,* 1967, Oct., no. 10, p. 836.
14. Nancy Dean, *In the Mind of the Writer,* San Francisco, CA: Canfield Press, 1973, p. 5.
15. Stanley Bradshaw, "Speaking Versus Writing," *Today's Speech,* vol. V, no. 3, p. 17.
16. Dean, p. 5.
17. Bradshaw, p. 18.
18. Andrew Wilkinson, *The Foundations of Language,* London, England: Oxford Univ. Press, 1971, pp. 47-48.
19. Bradshaw, p. 18.
20. Wilkinson, p. 48.
21. Louis Nizer, *Thinking on your Feet,* New York, NY: Pyramid Books, 1963, p. 22.

22. Nizer, p. 21.
23. G. A. Miller, "The Magical Number seven, plus or minus two: Some Limits on our Capacity for Processing Information," *Psychological Review,* 1956, 63, pp. 81-97.
24. Ornstein and Ehrlich, p. 5.
25. Ralph Y. Sasson and Paul Fraisse, "Images in Memory for Concrete and Abstract Sentences," *Journal of Experimental Psychology,* 1972, vol. 44, no. 2, p. 149.
26. R. B. Zajonc, "Feeling and Thinking: Preferences Need no Inferences," *American Psychologist,* 1980, vol. 35, p. 154.
27. Edward Levonian, *Effectiveness of Traffic Safety Films in Relation to Emotional Involvement,* Los Angeles, CA: Institute of Transportation and Traffic Engineering, Univ. of Calif., Los Angeles, 1965, p. 87.

III:12 AUDIENCE DECISION MAKING

1. Richard J. Lowry, ed., *Dominance, Self-Esteem, Self-Actualization: Germinal Papers of A. H. Maslow,* Monterey, CA: Brooks/Cole Pub. Co., 1973, p. 169.
2. Lowry, p. 171.
3. James A. Lee, *The Gold and the Garbage in Management Theories and Prescriptions,* Athens, OH: Ohio Univ. Press, 1980, pp. 69-70.
4. Lee, p. 69.
5. Lee, p. 96.
6. Lane Tracy, "Toward an Improved Need Theory: In Response to Legitimate Criticism," *Behavioral Science,* 1986, vol. 31, p. 205.
7. George Mandler, in Howard Gardner, *The Arts and Human Development,* New York, NY: John Wiley and Sons, Inc., 1973, p. 18.
8. George A. Kelly, *The Psychology of Personal Constructs,* New York, NY: W. W. Norton and Co., 1955, p. 46.
9. Mandler, pp. 111-112.
10. Wilder Penfield, in David Loye, *The Sphinx and the Rainbow,* Boulder Co: Shambhala Pub., Inc., 1983, p. 15.
11. Loye, p. 20.
12. A. R. Luria, *The Nature of Human Conflicts,* New York, NY: Washington Square Press, Inc., 1967, p. 378.

13. Martin E. Ford, *Motivating Humans,* Newbury Park, CA: Sage Pub., 1992, p. 6.
14. Irving L. Janis and Leon Mann, *Decision Making,* New York, NY: Houghton Mifflin Co., 1969, p. 132.
15. Aubry B. Fisher, "Decision Emergence: Phases in Group Decision Making," *Speech Monographs,* 1970, vol. 37, pp. 53-66.
16. Everett M. Rogers and Ronny Adhikarya, "Diffusion of Innovation: An Up-to-date-Review and Commentary," in *Communication Yearbook 3,* ed, Dan Nimmo, New Brunswick, NJ: International Communication Assoc., 1979, p. 75.
17. Ronald G. Havelock et al, *Planning for Innovation through Dissemination and Utilization of Knowledge,* Ann Arbor, MI: Institute for Social Research, Final Report Project No. 7-0028, Office of Education, 1969.
18. Beverly Byrum-Gaw, *It Depends: Appropriate Interpersonal Communication,* Sherman Oaks, CA: Alfred Pub. Co. Inc., 1961, p. 79.
19. Byrum-Gaw, p. 80
20. Joseph A. Ilardo, *Speaking Persuasively,* New York, NY: Macmillian Pub. Co., 1981, p. 117.
21. W. C. Helmhold and W. G. Rabinowitz, trans., Plato, *Phaedrus,* New York, NY: The Liberal Arts Press, 1956, St. 277.
22. William Stevenson, trans., Francois Fenelon, *Dialogue on Eloquence,* London: J. Moyes, 1808, p. 119.
23. Stevenson, p. 238.
24. M. M. Davy, *Sermons Universitaires Parisiens de 1230-1251,* Paris: Librairie Philosophique, 1931, p. 19.
25. Wilbur Samuel Howell, *Logic and Rhetoric in England 1500-1700,* Princton: Princton Univ. Press, 1956, pp. 344-345.
26. John Dewey, *How we Think,* Boston, MA: D. C. Heath and Co., 1910. Second Ed. 1933.
27. Dewey, pp. 115-116.
28. Ramon L. Irwin, "The Classical Speech Divisions," *The Quarterly Journal of Speech,* 25, 1939, p. 212.
29. Karl R. Wallace, *Francis Bacon on Communication,* Chapel Hill, NC: Univ. of North Carolina Press, 1943, p. 18.

III:13 PREPARATION AND DELIVERY STYLES

1. Roger Sperry, in David Galin, "Implications for Psychiatry of Left and Right Cerebral Specialization," *Archives of General Psychiatry,* 1974, no. 31, Oct., p. 573.
2. Galin, p. 573.
3. Paul Watzlawick, *The Language of Change,* New York, NY: Di Van Nostrand Co., 1971, p. 6.
4. Warren T. Norman, "...To Facilitate Learning," *Memo to the Faculty,* Ann Arbor, MI: Univ. of Michigan, Oct. 1979, p. 3.
5. Stanley M. Herman and Michael Korenich, *Authentic Management,* Reading, MA: Addison-Wesley Pub., Co., 1977, p. 3.
6. Josephine C. Moore, "Individual Differences and the Art of Therapy," *The American Journal of Occupational Therapy,* 1977, vol. 31, no. 10, p. 663.
7. Moore, p. 665.
8. Stephanie Winston, *The Organized Executive,* New York, NY: W. W. Norton and Co., 1983, p. 20.
9. David W. Ewing, "Discovering your Problem-solving Style," *Psychology Today,* 1977, Dec., p. 69.
10. Alfred G. Smith, *Cognitive Styles in Law Schools,* Austin, TX: Univ. of Texas Press, 1979, p. 131.
11. Smith, p. 132.

III:14 GETTING SUBJECTS

1. Paul D. Holtzman, *The Psychology of Speakers' Audiences,* Glenview, IL: Scott, Foresman and Col, 1970, p. 76.
2. Holtzman, p. 2.
3. Holtzman, p. 79.
4. Holtzman, p. 32.
5. Holtzman, p. 30.
6. Holtzman, p. 31.
7. Holtzman, p. 43.
8. Carl R. Rogers, *On Becoming a Person,* Boston, MA: Houghton Mifflin Co., 1951, pp. 26-7.
9. Robert P. Newman and Dale R. Newman, *Evidence,* Boston, MA: Houghton Mifflin Co., 1969, p. 132.
10. Newman and Newman, p. 151.

III:15 ORGANIZING PLANS

1. Luria, pp. 401-2.
2. Claude M. Steele and Thomas M. Ostrom, "Perspective-mediated Attitude Change: When is Indirect Persuasion More Effective than Direct Persuasion?" *Journal of Personality and Social Psychology,* 1974, no. 29, p. 135.
3. Gary Cronkhite, *Public Speaking and Critical Listening,* Menlo Park, CA: The Benjamin/Cummings Pub. Co. Inc., 1978, p. 38.
4. Edwin O. Reischaurer, *The Japanese,* Toyko, Japan: Charles E. Tuttle Co., 1977, p. 135.
5. Martin E. Ford, *Motivating Humans,* Newbury Park, CA: Sage Pub., 1992, p. 3.
6. Ford, p. 45.
7. Wheatley, p. 135.
8. E. H. Shattock, *An Experiment in Mindfulness,* London, England: Rider and Co., 1970, pp. 74-5.
9. Bernard Segal, et al., *Drugs, Day-Dreaming and Personality: A Study of College Youth,* Hillsdale, NJ: Lawrence Erlbaum Asoc., Pub., 1980, p. 30.
10. Segal, p. 32.
11. Segal, p. 34-5.
12. Segal, p. 217.
13. Charles B. Truax and Kevin M. Mitchell, "Research on Certain Therapist Interpersonal Skills in Relation to Process and outcome," p. 313, in Allen E. Bergin and Sol L. Garfield, *Handbook of Psychotherapy and Behavior Change: An Empirical Analysis,* New York, NY: John Wiley and Sons, Inc., 1971.
14. Richard, McKeon, trans., *The Basic Works of Aristotle,* New York, NY: Random House, 1941, p.14.
15. Wilkinson, p. 47-8.
16. Northrop Frye, *The Well-tempered Critic,* Bloomington, IN: Indiana Univ. Press, 1963, p. 18.

III:16 AIDING MEMORY

1. Thomas O. Nelson and Charles C. Hill, "Multiple Retreival Paths and Long-term Retention," *Journal of Experimental Psychology,* 1974, vol. 103, no. 1, pp. 185-187.
2. Fergus I. M. Craik and Michael J. Watkins, "The Role of

Rehearsal in Short-term Retention," *Journal of Verbal Learning and Verbal Behavior,* 1973, vol. 12, no. 6, pp. 599-607.

3. Richard M. Weist and Charlotte Crawford, "Sequential Versus Organized Rehearsal," *Journal of Experimental Psychology,* 1973, vol. 101, no. 2 pp. 237-241.
4. Lee Elliott, "Imagery Versus Repetition Encoding in Short and Long term Memory," *Journal of Experimental Psychology,* 1973, vol. 100, no. 2, pp. 270-276.
5. Ronald C. Peterson, "Imagery and Cued Recall: Concreteness or Content?" *Journal of Experimental Psychology,* 1974, vol. 41, no. 5, pp. 841-844.
6. Joseph Anderson, "Visualization and Verbalization as Mediators of Thought," *Speech Monographs,* 1974, vol. 41, no. 4, pp. 408-412.
7. K. Benson and I. Feinberg, "Sleep and Memory," *Psychophysiology,* 1975, vol. 12, no. 2, pp. 192-195.
8. Edward Levonian, "Retention of Information in Relation to Arousal during Continuously Presented Material," *American Educational Research Journal,* 1967, vol. 14, no. 2, p. 116.
9. Roland Fisher, "The Ectasy-Samedhi Continuum," *Philosophy Forum,* 1974, vol. 14, pp. 105-144.
10. Edward Jayne, "Psychostylistics: The Analysis of Short-term Retention Overload and its Effect upon Poetic Experience," unpublished paper, 1984, by permission.
11. Michael Osborn and Suzanne Osborn, *Public Speaking,* Boston, MA: Houghton Mifflin Co., 1991, p. 293.
12. "Best Memory: Both Word and Picture," *Science News,* 1978, vol.113, no. 8, Feb. 25, p. 122.
13. Vadim Deglin, "Our Split Brain," *The UNESCO Courier,* Jan. 1976.

III:17 LOWERING STRESS

1. Walter B. Cannon, *Bodily Changes in Pain, Hunger, Fear and Rage,* New York, NY: Appleton-Century-Crofts, 1929, pp. 193-194.
2. Magda Arnold, *Emotion and Personality, vol. II,* New York, NY: Columbia Univ. Press, 1960, p. 220.
3. Arnold, p. 224.
4. D. Thomas Porter, "Communication Apprehension.

Communication's Latest Artifact?" in *Communication Yearbook 3,* ed., Dan Nimmo, New Brunswick, NJ: International Communication Assoc., P. 256.
5. Mandler, p. 131.
6. Samuel M. Turner and Deborah C. Beidel, "Empirically Derived Subtypes of Social Anxiety," *Behavior Therapy,* vol. 16, 1985, p. 390.
7. Theodore Clevinger Jr. and Thomas R. King, "A Factor Analysis of the Visible Symptoms of Stage Fright," *Speech Monographs,* vol. 28, no. 4, 1961, p. 296.
8. Thomas D. Borkovec, "Physiological and Cognitive Processes in the Regulation of Anxiety," in *Consciousness and Self-regulation,* ed., Gary E. Schwartz and David Shapiro, New York, NY: Plenum Press, 1976, pp. 300-301.
9. Daniel H. Funkenstein, Stanley H. King and Margaret E. Drolette, *Mastery of Stress,* Cambridge, MA: Harvard Univ. Press, 1957, p. 274.
10. Hans Selye, *The Stress of Life,* New York, NY: Columbia Univ. Press, 1960, p. 118.
11. Selye, p. 98.
12. Selye, p. 89.
13. J. A. Daley and J. C. McCrosky, eds., *Avoiding Communication: Shyness, Reticence, and Communication Apprehension,* Beverly Hills, CA: Sage, 1984.
14. Funkenstein, p. 274.
15. Funkenstein, p. 276.
16. Jacqueline A. Thompson, "The Image Doctors," *MBA,* Sep. 1977, p. 25.
17. Borkovec, in Schwartz and Shapiro, p. 267.
18. Donald Meichenbaum, "Toward a Cognitive Theory of Self-control," in *Consciousness and Self-regulation,* ed., Gary E. Schwartz and David Shapiro, New York, NY: Plenum Press, 1976, p. 243.
19. Gordon L. Paul, *Insight vs. Desensitization in Psychotherapy,* Stanford, CA: Stanford Univ. Press, 1966.
20. Russel M. Myers, "Validation of Systematic Desensitization of Speech Anxiety through Galvanic Skin Response," *Speech Monographs,* 1974, vol. 41, June, p. 23, and Theodore

Clevenger, Jr, "A Synthesis of Experimental Research in Stage Fright," *Quarterly Journal of Speech,* 1959, vol. 45, pp. 134-145.

III:18 SPEAKING

1. Keith R. St. Onge, *Creative Speech,* Belmont, CA: Wadsworth Pub. Co. Inc., 1964, p. 195.
2. St. Onge, p. 198.
3. St. Onge, pp. 42-43.
4. Karl H. Pribram, "The New Neurology and the Biology of Emotion: A Structural Approach," *American Psychologist,* 1967, Oct. no. 10.
5. Pribram, p. 836.
6. Pribram, p. 836.
7. Pribram, p. 836.
8. Pribram, p. 837.
9. J. Kevin Barge, *Leadership: Communication Skills for Organizations and Groups,* New York, NY: St. Martins Press, 1994, p. v.
10. Mehrabian and Wiener, pp. 109-114.
11. Loren D. Crane, "The Speech Improvement Chart: A New Approach to Public Speaking Assessment." Paper presented at the Speech Communication Association Convention, 1994.
12. Casandra L. Book, "Providing Feedback on Student Speeches: The Research on Effective Oral and Written Feedback Strategies." Paper presented at the Speech Communication Association Convention, 1983.
13. G. Wiseman and Larry Barker, "A Study of Peer Group Evaluation," *Southern Speech Journal,* 1975, vol. 31, pp. 132-138.

Directory of Professional Speech Coaches

There are of course many speech teachers who can give excellent advice. However, the following are members of the Professional Speakers Association who advertise as coaches in presentational skills.

NAME	ADDRESS	PHONE
Dilip R. Abayasekara, PhD, DTM	4902 Carlisle Mechanicsburg, PA 17055	(302)834-2385
Katherine Abbott	577 St. John St. Pleasanton, CA 94566	(510)484-0195
ZaLonya Allen, MA	27350 Southfield Rd.Southfield, MI 48076	(810)352-0509
Vera J. Ami, MA	98-151 Palimomi #210 Aiea, HI 96701	(808)533-2811
Richard Davis Amme	3507 Kittery Ct. Winston-Salem, NC 27104	(910)768-9435
Edward C. Anthony, ScD, MBA	48 Beach ST. North Haven, CT 06473	(203)234-8458
Ron Arden	3728 Dixon Pl. San Diego, CA 92107	(619)222-1499
Richard T. Arundel, FASP, MCIM, ALAM, FCII	37-39 Southgate St. Winchester, Hampshire S023 9EH ENGLAND	44-701-0701-611
Bob Bailey	528 Ashford Silver Spring, MD 20910	(800)707-3240
Patricia Ball, CSP, CPAE	9875 Northbridge St. Louis, MO 63124	(314)966-5452
Jim Barber	1101 Marcano Blvd. Ft. Lauderdale, FL 33322	(954)476-9252
Gloria F. Barnes	6065 Roswell Ste 2200 Atlanta, GA 30328	(770)395-7400
Judy Kaplan Baron	6046 Cornerstone #208 San Diego, CA 92121	(619)558-7400
Marilynn Barron	PO Box 25239 Rochester, NY 14625	(716)385-4455

Wayne E. Baughman, CT	3044 Lischer Ave., Cincinnati, OH 45211	(513)481-4428
J. Terryl "Bubba" Bechtol, CSP	339 Panferio Dr., Pensacola Beach, FL 32561	(423)428-9707
Joani Bedore, PhD	2230 S. 99, Tulsa, OK 74129	(918)828-7763
Christina M. Bergenholtz, MEd	93 Providence Grfton, MA 01519	(508)839-5139
Francine Berger, CSP	20 Hawkins Rd. Stony Brook, NY 11790	(516)751-8549
Susan Berkley	616 Palisade Englewood Cliffs, NJ 07632	(201)541-8595
Frederick L. Berns	394 Rendezvous Dr. Lafayette, CO 80026	(303)665-6688
Annette F. Besignano	3310 Leisure World Silver Spring, MD 20906	(301)650-7493
Jeffrey Black, APR	414 Major Dr. Manning, SC 29102	(800)806-5656
Linda S. Blackman	5020 Castleman St. Pittsburgh, PA 15232	(412)682-2200
Ann Bloch	73 Birchwood Ln. Lenox, MA 01240	(413)637-0958
Gloria Boileau	PO Box 502 Cardiff, CA 92007	(760)730-0150
Dianna Booher, MA, CSP	4001 Gateway Dr. Colleyville, TX 76034	(817)318-6521
Sharon L. Bowman, MA	PO Box 464 Glenbrook, NV 89413	(702)749-5247
Bob Boylan, CSP	0129 Alexander Av. Snowmass, CO 81654	(970)927-9136
Ken Bradford	5990 Arapaho #18H Dallas, TX 75248	(972)233-9484
Elizabeth Brazell Nichols, MA	19 Concord Austin, TX 78737	(512)288-1095
Marjorie Brody, CSP, CMC	PO Box 8868 Elkins Park, PA 19027	(800)726-7936
David A. Brooks	6300 Wallace Cove Austin, TX 78750	(512)343-0111
Mark C. Budzinski	9842 Brie Ct Portland, OR 97229	(503)203-1422
John D. Cantu	1909 Lake St. #6 San Francisco, CA 94121	(415)668-2402
Bob Case, MA, DTM	2379 Bellaire St. Denver, CO 80207	(303)321-7464
Jim Cathcart, CSP, CPAE	PO Box 9075 La Jolla, CA 92038	(800)222-4883
C. Leslie Charles, CSP	PO Box 956 East Lansing, MI 48826	(517)675-7535
Rosa Chillis, M.Ed.	PO Box 35506 Detroit, MI 48235	(313)345-5481
Patricia A. Cohen-Hadria, MA	8845 Wine Valley Cir San Jose, CA 95135	(408)532-0502
Candice M. Coleman, PhD	1822 Hickory St. Louis, MO 63104	(314)621-9228

Brian Collins	527 N Acacia Solana Beach, CA 92075	(800)776-5376
Loren D. Crane, PhD	5175 Driftwood Kalamazoo MI 49009	(616)375-3927
John Creighton	PO Box 128 Middleburg, VA 20118	(540)687-3255
Graham Davies	4 Marzell House, 120 North End Rd. London W14 9PP ENGLAND	44-171-381-8691
Zita M. Johnson De Faria	AL. Budapeste 375-Alphaville Zero Barueri, SP 06475-270 BRAZIL	55-11-7295-6420
Roland De Rose	1521 Tejana Mesa Albuquerque, NM 87112	(505)856-8698
Patricia J. DeStefano	2 Peter Cooper Rd.#3H New York, NY 10010	(212)260-4093
Robert Dickman	1551 11th Santa Monica, CA 90401	(310)394-8829
Walter Dickman, CSP	61 Bocks Oakville NSW 2765 AUSTRALIA	+61029-627-1227
Diane DiResta	PO Box 140714 Staten Island, NY 10314	(718)273-8627
Patrick J. Donadio, MBA	191 W. Jeffrey Pl. Columbus, OH 43214	(614)263-3421
Burt Dubin	1 Speaking Success Rd. Kingman, AZ 86402	(520)753-7546
Dee Dukehart	PO Box 100331 Denver, CO 80250	(303)220-1094
Elaine C. Dumler	1244 Ceres Dr. Lafayette, CO 80026	(303)665-5391
Gerry Felski	24 Windsor Merrimack, NH 03054	(603)424-1979
Molly Finn	38 Washburn Av. Needham, MA 02192	(617)449-1186
Graham H. Foster, CSP	PO Box 1059 Carindale Qld 4152 AUSTRALIA	+61073893
Jane E. Foster	10455 Cen. Expressway Dallas, TX 75231	(214)373-8075
Sharon D. Frank, MA, CCC-SLP	79 Oak Foxboro, MA 02035	(508)698-3709
Anne B. Freedman	1541 Sunset #210 Coral Gables, FL 33143	(305)669-1449
Patricia Fripp, CSP, CPAE	527 Hugo St. San Francisco, CA 94122	(415)753-6556
Sue Gaulke	4261 Chamberlin Dr. Hood River, OR 97031	(541)354-2902
John K. Gilday	22 Maguire Av. Staten Island, NY 10309	(718)984-5549
Lee Glickstein	20 Sunnyside A107 Mill Valley, CA 94941	(415)381-8044
Sandy Goodwin, RN, PHN	3144 N G #125-144 Merced, CA 95340	(209)384-7996
Alan Grishman, PhD	5545 Aylesboro Pittsburgh, PA 15217	(412)621-1994
Corey Hansen, MFA, AEA	7304 N Bellefontaine Kansas City, MO 64119	(816)436-8748
Mark Victor Hansen, CSP	PO Box 7665 Newport Beach, CA 92658	(800)433-2314

Mary Jane Hartigan	60 Walnut Ln. Manhasset, NY 11030	(516)627-0275
H. Tony Hartmann	8225 Conarroe Rd. Indianapolis, IN 46278	(317)876-8304
Jean Palmer Heck	1955 Mulsanne Dr. Zionsville, IN 46077	(317)873-3772
Kathleen Hessert, CSP	2700 Coltsgate Rd. Charlotte, NC 28211	(704)365-5027
Gordon Hill	PO Box 21137 St. Petersburg, FL 33742	(813)576-4028
Ralph E. Hillman, PhD	MTSU Box 373 Murfreesboro, TN 37132	(615)898-2271
Rosemary, Horner, MS	31 Oakland Irvington, NJ 07111	(973)399-7454
Marcy L. Huber	7F #2 Yen Chi Alley 6 Lane 62 HSI CHIH Taipei 106 TAIWAN-ROC	886227517797
Anita I. Jacobs, PhD, CSP	1504 Jefferson St. Teaneck, NJ 07666	(800)671-8255
Tony Jeary	3001 LBJ Freeway #240 Dallas, TX 75234	(972)484-9627
Sheri Jeavons	6557 Cross Creek Trail Brecksville, OH 44141	(216)526-4400
June Johnson, DMA	500 W Bender Rd.#67 Milwaukee, WI 53217	(414)332-0926
Frank Jonasson	PO Box 600083 San Diego, CA 92160	(800)296-3765
Dolores W. Jones	1043 Bell Av. Landsdowne, PA 19050	(610)259-5048
Janet Jordan	PO Box 290 Cambridge, MA 02238	(617)643-7735
C. Mike Jousan	8355 E McDonald Dr. Scottsdale, AZ 85250	(800)544-9551
Betska G. L. K-Burr	50 Beechfern Stittsville, ON K2S 1E3 CANADA	(613)831-8933
Ellen A. Kaye	PO Box 6064 Scottsdale, AZ 85261	(602)391-9888
Kay D. Keller	150 Hibiscus Punta Gorda, FL 33950	(941)575-0768
Colleen Kettenhofen, BFA	32460 Crown Vly Pky Dana Point, CA 92629	(714)493-7239
Samantha Koumanelis	1016 George Hill Rd. Lancaster, MA 01523	(978)368-0801
Julie Krivanek, MSS	1077 Race St. Ste. 701 Denver, CO 80206	(303)377-0705
Eileen G. Kugler	6807 Bluecurl Cir Springfield, VA 22152	(703)644-3039
Karen Lake	28532 Chimney Rock Portola Hills, CA 92679	(949)888-8441
Lenny J. Laskowski	106 Schoolhouse Rd.Newington, CT 06111	(800)606-4855
John W. Lawson	8740 Seminole Blvd. Seminole, FL 33722	(813)392-7720
Thomas Leech	4901 Morena #102A San Diego, CA 92117	(619)274-5668
Leonard J. Lipton, PhD	PO Box 1498 Santa Monica, CA 90406	(310)451-5670
Leslie K.A. Lorette	43A Glengowan Rd. Toronto, ON M4N 1G1 CANADA	(416)488-0074
Sidney Madwed	215 Crest Terrace Fairfield, CT 06432	(203)372-6484

Mary Jane Mapes, CSP	7735 Angling Rd. Kalamazoo, MI 49024	(616)324-1847
Shirley Markley	PO Box 161842 Austin, TX 78716	(512)329-0881
Adrienne B. Marks	4 Clubside Dr Woodmere, NY 11598	(516)569-6101
Mary A. McGlynn	200 B Twin Dophin Dr. Redwood City, CA 94065	(650)631-8459
James N. Morrison	PO Box 10801 Green Bay, WI 54307	(920)434-4540
Thomas E. Mungaven	5850 Opus Pkwy Minnetonka, MN 55343	(800)242-6431
Elizabeth Ann Myers	PO Box 1526 Princton, NJ 08542	(609)737-6832
Cheri Najor-Parks, MSW	PO Box 7668 Bloomfield Hills, MI 48302	(248)335-2885
Vanna H. Novak	1909 32nd Av. W Seattle, WA 98199	(206)284-8336
Marilyn S. Nyman, MEd, CCC	200 Lakeside Dr. Horsham, PA 19044	(215)956-0300
Karla L. Oard	2300 Jefferson Grand Rapids, MI 49507	(616)248-3736
Susam H. Ogle	36 Highland Rd. Charlestown, RI 02813	(401)322-9823
Ramona Ann Parris, MPA	2020 Wenlok Trail Marietta, GA 30066	(770)928-8400
Maureen O. Pearce	PO Box 36100 Christchurch 8030 NEW ZEALAND	64-3-359-8232
Randy G. Pennington, CSP	4004 Winter Park Ln Dallas, TX 75244	(972)980-9857
Carol C. Peterson	3901 SW 22nd Dr. Gresham, OR 97080	(503)666-7733
Pamela Peterson	2972 Windcrest Way Grand Rapids, MI 49525	(616)787-1041
Hugh C. Phillips	11026 - 126 St. NW Edmonton AB T5M OP7 CANADA	(403)455-7219
Judith Pollock	4115 Wisconsin Av. NW Wash. DC 20016	(202)363-4521
David Julian Price, CSP	PO Box 463 Jolimont WA 6913 AUSTRALIA	+610893839499
Mary J. Pryor	PO Box 851435 Yukon, OK 73085	(405)354-1604
Jack Pyle	1800 N Meridian Mason, MI 48854	(800)395-7953
Beverly Carlson Quinn	PO Box 7515 McLean, VA 22106	(703)356-7844
Kai Rambow	90 Cordova Av. #1214 Islington, ON M9A 2H8 CANADA	(416)231-2718
Caterina Rando, MA	182 22nd Av San Franciscio, CA 94121	(800)966-3603
Karen Lynn Ray	PO Box 1787 Aspen, CO 81612	(970)928-6630
Michelle Ray	314-1075 W 14th Av. Vancouver, BC V6H 1P4 CANADA	(604)736-3090
C. Ann Reed	4130 Winding Creek Sacramento, CA 95864	(916)973-1492

Marlena Reigh	2359 Prarie Ann Arbor, MI 48105	(313)668-6074
J. Michael Reilly, MA	7855 W. US Hwy 2 Naubinway, MI 49762	(906)292-0065
Karen Cortell Reisman, MS	13210 Laurel Wood Ln. Dallas, TX 75240	(972)490-8676
Clare Rice	PO Box 12848 Tallahassee, FL 32317	(850)893-3537
Diane P. Ripstein, MEd	155 Grant Av. Newton Centre, MA 02159	(617)630-8630
Ted Ritsick	421 N Penn Av Wilkes-Barre, PA 18702	
Mary Beth Roach, MA	18020 Bal Harbour Dr. Houston, TX 77058	(281)333-3558
Jo Robbins, CSP	5900 Upper Bremo Ln. New Albany, OH 43054	(614)939-1300
Jan M. Roelofs	2218 1st Av. NE Cedar Rapids, IA 52402	(319)363-6005
Rosemarie Rossetti, PhD	1008 Eastchester Dr. Columbus, OH 43230	(614)471-6100
Heidi B. Rothfels, MBA	74 Malvern Av. Ste. 200 Toronto, ON M4E 3E3 CANADA	(416)698-7755
Sandra Schrift	10151 Grandview Dr. La Mesa, CA 91941	(619)460-7866
Linda B. Shields, MS, CCC-SLP	PO Box 874 Hope Mills, NC 28348	(910)425-6253
Shelley Siu	Unit 21 Elliot Rd 458703, SINGAPORE	(65) 444-7300
Gloria Sitzman	6 Hastings Rd. Lexington, MA 02173	(781)863-1651
Terri L. Sjodin	PO Box 8998 Fountain Valley, CA 92728	(714)540-5594
Dennis Stauffer	PO Box 46021 Minneapolis, MN 55446	(612)473-9763
Marilyn A. Snyder, MS	2533 Thorn Pl. Fullerton, CA 92835	(714)961-8930
Phillip J. Stella, MS	6459 Derby Dr. Mayfield Village, OH 44143	(440)449-0356
Barbara Stellard	PO Box 5058 N Muskegon, MI 49445	(616)744-4771
Douglas B. Stewart	4111 Chestnut St. Fairfax, VA 22030	(703)277-9782
Susan D. St. John	6424 San Bonita Av. Clayton, MI 63105	(314)725-1595
Mary Ann Stilgoe	15 Cottage Ave. Quincy, MA 02169	(617)773-2302
Roseann Sullivan, MA	1777 Shoreline Dr. Alameda, CA 94501	(510)521-6700
Bill R. Swetmon	2005 Midcrest Dr. Plano, TX 75075	(972)422-1274
George Torok	3211 Maderna Rd. Burlington, ON L7M 2V6 CANADA	(905)335-1997
Joyce Turley, MEd, CSP	98 Main St. Tiburon, CA 94920	(415)435-3875
Terry Van Tell	155 W. 68 St., Ste. 30B New York, NY 10023	(212)874-1453
Mari Pat Varga	4939 N Winchester Chicago, IL 60640	(773)989-7348
Janie Walters	2325 Jones St. Gulfport, MS 39507	(601)896-1336

Karl E. Walinskas, PE	421 N. Penn Av. Wilkes-Barre, Pa 18702	(717)675-8956
Wendy Warman, MS	314 S Missouri Av. Clearwater, FL 33756	(813)441-9858
Diane L. Westbrook, MS	1816 Jonquil NW Olympia, WA 98502	(360)352-4857
Sam Wieder, NLP	860 Harrison City #5A Greensburg, PA 15601	(724)832-7459
Reesa Woolf	3711 Seven Mile Ln. Baltimore, MD 21208	(800)769-6653
Terry-Lynn Zietsman-Fendt	PO Box 948 Umhlanga Rocks Durban, Natal 4320 SOUTH AFRICA	27-31-561-2689
Sandra Zimmer, MA	11221 Richmond Av. Houston, TX 77082	(713)785-2909
Anthony Joseph Zino	2000 Powers Ferry Ste. 300 Marietta, GA 30067	(770)857-8353

Toastmasters International

Reading books can give you great insights into speech preparation and presentation, but the only way you will ever become a dynamic, persuasive speaker is through practice and feedback. A Toastmasters club can help you.

Since the nonprofit educational organization was founded in 1924, more than three million men and women have benefited from its programs. There are now 175,000 members in 8,400 clubs in 65 countries throughout the world.

How it works

A typical Toastmasters club has 20 members who meet weekly or biweekly to practice public speaking techniques using instructional materials provided by Toastmasters International. At each club meeting you speak in front of others and your audience then offers constructive feedback on your efforts. Besides taking turns delivering prepared speeches and evaluating other's speeches, members give impromptu talks on assigned topics, usually related to current events. They also develop listening skills, conduct meetings, learn parliamentary procedure, and gain leadership experience by serving as club officers. But most importantly, they develop self-confidence.

The benefits of Toastmasters' proven and simple learning formula have not been lost on the thousands of corporations that sponser in-house Toastmasters clubs as cost-efficient means of satisfying their employees' needs for communication training. Toastmasters clubs can be found in the U.S. Senate and the House of Representatives as well as in a variety of community organizations, prisons, universities, hospitals, military bases, and churches.

How to get started

Most cities in North America have several Toastmasters clubs that meet at different times and locations during the week. If you are interested in forming or joining a club, call 1 (800) 9WESPEAK, visit the web site www.toastmasters.org, or write to Toastmasters International, PO Box 9052, Mission Viejo, CA 92690.

Word Index

Action speech 30, 124
Argument speech 30, 116-24
Attention factors 5, 71
Awareness speech 30, 113-16
Conclusion 10, 38, 134
Correlation 31, 38, 97, 141
Decision cycle 13
Decision making stages 11, 82
Deductive 22, 31, 92, 99
Delivery notes 45-6, 56, 146
Demographic analysis 20, 24, 99
80-20 principle 2, 67, 72
Ethics 2, 67-8
Ideas 20, 38, 43-5, 101, 130, 133, 144
Imagery 20, 44-6, 101, 126-27, 130, 133, 144
Inductive 23, 31, 92, 99
Information speech 30, 116
Impromptu speech 40, 141
Introduction 10, 37, 131
Language 7, 48, 66, 73-7, 134, 151, 179
Memory 8, 44, 77, 143, 152
Need-motivation 11, 79
Oratory 39, 139
Outline, idea-imagery 35-6, 130
Outline, logical 29, 34-5, 111
Passive delivery 56, 170
Perception 6, 72
Preparation uniformity 15, 91
Preview 10, 37, 132
Review 10, 38, 134
Rhetoric xiv, 1, 65, 67-8, 73, 85
Rote rehearsal 44, 143
Selection 32, 38, 141
Sequence 30, 38, 97, 140
Social science 1, 66
Speech cycle 3, 69
Speech format 10, 37-8, 78, 131
Speech nucleus 20, 101
Speech progress chart 60-62, 180-81, 207
Speech stress 50, 158-63
Speech subject label 22, 101
Stage fright 50, 153-58
Thinking styles 2, 15, 94
Visual aid(s) 47, 148-50
Word probes 24-5, 105-6

Name Index

Antiphon 87
Appolodorus 86
Aristotle 85-6, 131
Ashby 173
Blunderville 88
Book 180
Borkovec 158
Buddah 126
Campbell 73
Cannon 153, 159
Churchill ix
Claude 88
Clevinger and King 158
Confucius 126
Corax 87
Descartes 88
Dewey 88
Emerson ix
Fabri 87
Fenelon 87
Fisher 83
Freud 79
Frye 139
Funkenstein 161
Gorgias 85
Hermocrates 87
Herzberg 80
Ilardo 85
Isocrates 87
Jayne 144
Jesus 126
Kelly 81
Kennedy xv
Kierkegaard 125
Lap-tze 126
Luria 81, 125
Lysias 87
Maslow 79
McKenny and Keen 96
Mehrabian and Wiener 73, 180
Milner 147
Monroe 89
Myers-Briggs 97
Pareto 66
Paul 166
Penfield 81
Plato 85-7
Protagoras 86
Ramee 87
Rogers 103
Solzhenitsyn 68
Sophists 85-6
Sperry 91

Theodorus 86-7
Von Restorff 9, 78
Wiseman and Barker 181
Zenker 162

SPEECH PROGRESS CHART

Speaker__________ Subject __________ Rater __________ Grade__________

For each speaking variable, mark the quality of the speaking behavior on a scale from D to A. If the behavior changes, place a second mark and draw an arrow to it.

DELIVERY

	D	C	B	A
1. Beginning	Weak	Average	Good	Strong
2. Movement	Random/lean	Poised	Pacing	Varied
3. Gesture	Random	None	Few	Many
			Weak	Strong
			Repetitious	Varied
Distraction	Physical			
4. Eye-contact	Little	Half time	Good	Continual
5. Loudness	Weak	Average	Good	Projection
6. Sounds	Read	Average	Well	First time
	Memorized	Average	Well	
7. Pace	Rushed	Fast	Good	Varied
	Hesitations	Jerky		
	Drags	Slow		
Distraction	Vocal			
8. Ending	Weak	Average	Good	Strong
9. Time	Over			Well timed
	Under			
	D	C	B	A

CONTENT

	D	C	B	A
1. Intro. (why)	Negative	Abrupt	Good	Relevant
2. Preview (what)	None	Brief	Ideas	Prominent
			Purpose	Prominent
3. Form	Written	Average	Good	Conversational
4. Language	Vague/slang	Average	Good Explanation	Precise
			Good Description	Vivid
5. Transitions	None	Brief	Good	Prominent
6. Source	None cited	Personal	Good	Expert
		Popular	Good	Authority
7. Purpose	Weak awareness	Average	Good	New priority
	Weak information	Average	Good	New belief
	Weak argument	Average	Good	New attitude
	Weak action	Average	Good	New behavior
8. Review (what)	None	Brief	Idea summary	Prominent
			Purpose summary	Prominent
9. Conc. (why)	Negative	Abrupt	Good	Relevant
	D	C	B	A

SPEECH PROGRESS CHART

Speaker________________ Subject ________________ Rater __________ Grade______

For each speaking variable, mark the quality of the speaking behavior on a scale from D to A. If the behavior changes, place a second mark and draw an arrow to it.

DELIVERY

	D	C	B	A
1. Beginning	Weak	Average	Good	Strong
2. Movement	Random/lean	Poised	Pacing	Varied
3. Gesture	Random	None	Few	Many
			Weak	Strong
			Repetitious	Varied
Distraction	Physical			
4. Eye-contact	Little	Half time	Good	Continual
5. Loudness	Weak	Average	Good	Projection
6. Sounds	Read	Average	Well	First time
	Memorized	Average	Well	
7. Pace	Rushed	Fast	Good	Varied
	Hesitations	Jerky		
	Drags	Slow		
Distraction	Vocal			
8. Ending	Weak	Average	Good	Strong
9. Time	Over			Well timed
	Under			
	D	C	B	A

CONTENT

	D	C	B	A
1. Intro. (why)	Negative	Abrupt	Good	Relevant
2. Preview (what)	None	Brief	Ideas	Prominent
			Purpose	Prominent
3. Form	Written	Average	Good	Conversational
4. Language	Vague/slang	Average	Good Explanation	Precise
			Good Description	Vivid
5. Transitions	None	Brief	Good	Prominent
6. Source	None cited	Personal	Good	Expert
		Popular	Good	Authority
7. Purpose	Weak awareness	Average	Good	New priority
	Weak information	Average	Good	New belief
	Weak argument	Average	Good	New attitude
	Weak action	Average	Good	New behavior
8. Review (what)	None	Brief	Idea summary	Prominent
			Purpose summary	Prominent
9. Conc. (why)	Negative	Abrupt	Good	Relevant
	D	C	B	A